FOREWORD

In March 1975 the OECD published a Report "Re-appraisal of Regional Policies in OECD Countries". The report was a comprehensive analytical survey of the main aspects of regional policies as they have been pursued in member countries. It reviewed the nature of regional problems in general, the types and methods of policies adopted and the problems which experience has shown to be associated with the development of regional policies.

The present report examines the situation as it has developed - and seems likely to develop, in a number of individual countries. The two reports taken together are intended to serve as a comprehensive analytical and descriptive survey, covering general principles and the way they are applied in individual countries.

Together they constitute a major phase of the work of the Organisation on regional policies - through its Working Party No 6 of the Industry Committee - and reflect the results of continuing study by the Working Party over a number of years.

The present report is arranged in 'country by country' order, but each country chapter is presented in similar structure, viz:

- The national perspective of regional problems.
- The emergence of regional problems and their nature.
- The development of the approach to regional policies.
- The instruments of regional policies.
- The development of methodology.
- Conclusions drawn from experience.
- Expectations.

The countries treated in the present volume are: France, Italy, Ireland, Denmark, Sweden and Japan. Chapters on other countries will be issued subsequently in a companion volume.

November, 1975

REGIONAL PROBLEMS AND POLICIES IN OECD COUNTRIES

VOLUME I

France - Italy - Ireland
Denmark - Sweden - Japan

ORGANISATION FOR ECONOMIC CO-OPERATION AND DEVELOPMENT

The Organisation for Economic Co-operation and Development (OECD) was set up under a Convention signed in Paris on 14th December, 1960, which provides that the OECD shall promote policies designed:
— to achieve the highest sustainable economic growth and employment and a rising standard of living in Member countries, while maintaining financial stability, and thus to contribute to the development of the world economy;
— to contribute to sound economic expansion in Member as well as non-member countries in the process of economic development;
— to contribute to the expansion of world trade on a multilateral, non-discriminatory basis in accordance with international obligations.

The Members of OECD are Australia, Austria, Belgium, Canada, Denmark, Finland, France, the Federal Republic of Germany, Greece, Iceland, Ireland, Italy, Japan, Luxembourg, the Netherlands, New Zealand, Norway, Portugal, Spain, Sweden, Switzerland, Turkey, the United Kingdom and the United States.

TABLE OF CONTENTS

I

FRANCE

A. THE NATIONAL PERSPECTIVE

The population of France, estimated at 51.7 million for 1972
increased by about 7 million between 1954 and 1968 and by about
2 million since 1968. The annual average growth rate for the decade to
1972 was 0.96% (cf United Kingdom of 0.45%, Italy 0.67%, Germany
0.82%, Spain 1.04%, Japan 1.10%). The active population (numbers
employed), estimated for 1972 at 20.7 million, increased in the same
periods by 1.1 million and 1.8 million respectively. The economy
has expanded considerably more than proportionately ; G.D.P. at 1963
market prices rose, in the decide 1961 - 70 from 365 thousand million
francs to 607 thousand million, or by two-thirds.

These global changes reflected marked structural changes. There
was a substantial decline in agricultural employment, which fell by
2 million, from 5 million to 3 million, between 1954 and 1968 and to
2.5 million in 1972. By contrast industrial employment rose by more
than 1 million between 1954 and 1968 and continued to rise, at a slower
pace in subsequent uears. The tertiary sector expanded still more,
increasing by 2.3 million from 1962-72 while employment in construction rose by 0.4 million in the same decade. In 1962 the proportions
employed in agriculture and industry were 20% and 30% respectively.
In 1973 they were 12.2% and 39.3%.

Of the increase in G.D.P. in the decade 1961-70, amounting to 232
thousand million francs at 1963 prices, manufacturing accounted for
100 thousand million, construction for 27 thousand million and whole-
sale and retail trade for 27 thousand million, transport and communications for 12 thousand million, public administration and defence for
11 thousand million and agriculture for 7.1 thousand million, manufacturing being in this respect by far the largest single contributor,
rising as a proportion from 35.4% to 37.8% of the total.

In terms of G.D.P. and civilian employment the French economy
can be said to have been one of constant expansion rather than subject
to major swings. In each of the years 1961-70 for example both
G.D.P. and civilian employment rose year by year (except in 1968
when there was a slight fall in the latter index). Unemployment was
well below 1% of the labour force in each year until 1968, but rose
above this level first in 1968 increasing to around 2% in subsequent
years.

The maintenance of a high level of demand for labour has been a factor in the maintenance of a high rate of immigration, to a peak of 860,000 net in 1962 and of the order of over 100,000 in each of the years 1962 to 1972.

The expansion of the economy has resulted not only from the growth in the labour supply but also in its productivity, averaging about 5% p.a. between 1960 and 1970 and over 6% in the industrial sector. The predictions in the VIth Plan were for increases of 5.4% and 7% respectively in 1970-75. Of great significance also to the development of the French economy was its participation in the EEC, increasing the influence of international factors and requiring a continuing adaptation to the conditions of international, particularly European competition.

The picture thus presented is (until recently) of a strong and expanding economy in which considerable structural readjustment, particularly through the decline in the importance of agriculture and the growth in industry and tertiary employment has been necessary and effectively brought about.

B. THE EMERGENCE OF REGIONAL PROBLEMS AND THEIR NATURE

The experience of all countries in which the economy expands and at the same time undergoes structural change, involving the rise of some industries and the decline of others is that change is not spread evenly throughout the country. France is no exception to this rule. Change occurs geographically, in that certain areas or regions have conditions favourable to the growth industries while others have a higher proportion of the industries which decline. Changes in the techniques of industry, in their employment ratios, in productivity, compounded with changes in means of transport and communication, social composition and skills, income levels and consumption habits and preferences, also alter the location requirements and preferences of industry and affect the degree of urbanisation and the urban/rural balance in the geographical distribution of population. As has been explained more fully in the Re-appraisal of Regional Policies in OECD Countries* regional problems arise essentially out of this complex process of change which produces unevenness and imbalances in the development of a country in regional terms.

The French regional situation is more or less a classic illustration of these general principles. Three main elements are of particular importance in describing the regional situation:

---

*   Referred to hereafter as the "Re-appraisal".

i)   The decline in agricultural employment

Agricultural employment halved between 1954 and 1972.   The
rate of decline has been of the order of 3.5% per annum or 130,000
in the period of the Vth Plan (1966-70) and is estimated in the VIth
Plan (1971-75) to continue at the rate of 100,000 per annum.   This
decline affects especially the Western half of France.   Two thirds
of the farming population live in these regions which are deemed to
be in a particularly critical situation, being under-populated, under-
industrialised and under-equipped, having few towns and an average
income per household well below that found in the more highly industrialised regions of the country.   The decline in agricultural employment, resulting in part from improved technology, changes in size of
farms and in markets has both economic and social effects.

In economic terms manpower is released but must find alternative
employment locally or elsewhere (involving migration); social, in
changing the age structure of the employed population and the "quality
of life" in rural areas.   The importance traditionally attached in
France to agriculture and country life creates social as well as economic
problems, and places adjustment to agricultural change in the forefront
of the French "regional problem".

ii)   Decline in other basic industries, particularly coal mining

Change in productivity and the greater utilisation of other energy
sources (oil, hydroelectric and nuclear power) have led to a marked
decline in employment in coal mining.   Numbers employed in mining
and quarrying as a whole fell from 369,000 to 193,000 between 1957
and 1971.

Here again the regional impact is uneven, owing to the particular
geographical situation of the coal mining areas.   The main areas
affected are the coal fields in the Centre, and the Midi (South) -
(St. Etienne, Alès, Mure, Auvergne) areas remote from the industrial
regions of Europe; the coal fields in the North (Pas-de-Calais in particular); and in Lorraine.

iii) The growth of the Paris region

The Paris region constitutes 2.2% (or one fiftieth) of the surface
area of France.   In 1954 it had about one sixth of the population of
France (7.3 million out of 42.8 million).   By the 1968 census its population had risen to 9.2 million out of 49.6 million (18%).   The forecast
for 1976 in the VIth Plan is for 10.3 million out of 53.8 million (19%).
Over a longer historical period, from 1901 to 1962 while the population
of France increased by 70% that of the Paris region multiplied six-fold.

This degree of concentration, and the continued tendency to relative
growth, have long been deemed as unacceptable in France.   Even though
it may result from the economic advantage which the Paris region can

offer, and from the tendency to growth in the industrial and tertiary sectors there are offsetting disadvantages, the physical and social problems connected with urban congestion-overcrowding, high cost infrastructure and strain on social services. Of social and political importance is the imbalance in the regional structure of France created by the excessive concentration of the institutions of higher education and research and the higher professional and technical skills resulting in the region having a disproportionate share of the higher income occupations.

The problem of urban growth, which is the counterpart of rural decline, is compounded by the excessive concentration and growth of the Paris region which enhances the dominating role of the capital in the life of France as a whole. The tendencies which have led to this situation are self sustaining, feeding on themselves. If unchecked, the Paris region could be expected to absorb an even larger proportion of the nation's population and assets in future and produce a progressive imbalance in the regional structure of the country as a whole. How to ensure that this trend is adequately diminished constitutes the core of the problem for regional policy and is connected with that of securing a better regional balance in the process of the continued expansion of the economy which can be foreseen.

Though the three elements define the more specific features of change which delineate the main regional problems, other important changes in the regional structure are noteworthy. Tables 1-3 show the way in which population, migratory flows and numbers employed have become redistributed between the 22 "programme regions" since 1954 and up to 1976 (as envisaged within the VIth Plan). A map showing the programme regions is also given.

The following figures, derived from Table 1, show the importance and the continuous growth in population of the high density regions:

REGIONS	GROWTH 1954-68
Paris	1.9 million
Rhône-Alpes	0.8 million
Provence-Côte-d'Azur	0.9 million
North	0.4 million
Lorraine	0.3 million
	4.3 million

The remaining 17 regions grew in total only 2.6 million, regions of the West show particularly slow growth :

REGIONS	GROWTH 1954-68
Brittany	0. 1 million
Loire	0. 3 million
Poitou-Charentes	0. 1 million
Aquitaine	0. 3 million
Auvergne	0. 7 million
Midi-Pyrénées	0. 2 million
	1. 7 million

The Limousin actually declined.

Table 2 shows net migratory flows of population by region between periods from 1954 to 1968. In the first period (1954-62) there were net outward flows in 8 regions, and in the second period (1962-68) in 7. In the first period they were particularly large in Brittany, Lower Normandy, Poitou-Charentes and the North; in the second period in Lorraine, the North and Poitou-Charentes. Conversely, inward flows were exceptionally large in the Paris region, Rhone-Alpes and Provence-Côte d'Azur.

The trends in the two periods were not uniform. In 1962-68 the negative trend (net outflow) was reversed in Picardy and Champagne-Ardennes, Limousin and Auvergne. In Lower-Normandy, Loire and especially Brittanny the negative trend diminished, while in Poitou-Charentes it remained stable. On the other hand it became more marked in the North and worsened in Lorraine where a positive net flow became negative.

Table 3 indicates the movement of the employed working population between the three censuses and gives the forecast for the end of the VIth Plan. It should be noted that forecasts for both population and employment are somewhat arbitrary, based on assuptions concerning the aims of industrialising the West of France. They are also normative in that they are a criterion in the calculation of the five year Government loans allocated to the regions.

The table shows that, with the exception of the Paris region, Rhône-Alpes and Provence-Côte-d'Azur, a few regions bordering on the Paris region: Champagne, Picardy, Lorraine and Languedoc, all the other regions lost part of their working population between 1954 and 1962.

Some only returned to their former level of employment in 1968: Centre, Lower-Normandy, Burgundy, North, Alsace and Lorraine. In others the old level of employment should be restored by the end of the VIth Plan - Poitou-Charentes and Auvergne, while some-Brittany and Midi-Pyrénées - will still be behind even them.

1968, however, marked a turning point in the population trends.

(in '000)

Table 1. TOTAL POPULATION

REGIONS	SURFACE AREA %	1954 CENSUS	1962 CENSUS	1968 CENSUS	FORECASTS FOR 1.1.1976 (END OF VIth PLAN)
Paris Region	2.2	7,317	8,470	9,238	10,354
Champagne	4.7	1,134	1,206	1,279	1,382
Picardy	3.6	1,387	1,483	1,579	1,723
Upper Normandy	2.3	1,274	1,398	1,497	1,679
Centre	7.2	1,758	1,858	1,990	2,165
Lower Normandy	3.2	1,165	1,208	1,260	1,334
Burgundy	5.8	1,375	1,439	1,503	1,583
North	2.3	3,375	3,659	3,815	4,038
Lorraine	4.3	1,956	2,194	2,274	2,439
Alsace	1.5	1,218	1,318	1,412	1,570
Franche Comté	3.0	856	928	992	1,074
Pays de la Loire	5.9	2,319	2,462	2,581	2,735
Brittany	5.0	2,339	2,397	2,468	2,583
Poitou Charentes	4.8	1,394	1,451	1,481	1,532
Aquitaine	7.6	2,209	2,312	2,460	2,575
Midi Pyrénées	8.3	1,976	2,061	2,185	2,258
Limousin	3.0	740	734	736	747
Rhône Alpes	8	3,630	4,019	4,431	4,929
Auvergne	4.8	1,247	1,273	1,312	1,365
Languedoc	5.1	1,449	1,555	1,708	1,802
Provence Côte d'Azur	5.8	2,415	2,813	3,288	3,712
Corsica	1.6	247	176	209	232
Whole of France	100	42,780	46,414	49,698	53,811

SOURCE: Plan - INSEE.

12

Table 2. NET MIGRATORY FLOWS BY REGION

(between 1954-1962 and 1962-1968)

REGIONS	BALANCE OF MIGRATION		NET ANNUAL MIGRATORY FLOW (%)	
	1954-1962	1962-1968	1954-1962	1962-1968
Paris Region	+ 710,300	+ 365,400	+ 1.2	+ 0.7
Champagne Ardennes	- 9,400	+ 7,600	- 0.1	+ 0.1
Picardy	- 10,700	+ 18,600	- 0.1	+ 0.2
Upper Normandy	+ 9,500	+ 11,900	+ 0.1	+ 0.1
Centre	+ 20,400	+ 72,200	+ 0.1	+ 0.6
North	- 20,100	- 48,400	- 0.1	- 0.2
Lorraine	+ 50,500	- 69,300	+ 0.3	- 0.5
Alsace	+ 25,700	+ 36,700	+ 0.3	+ 0.5
Franche Comté	+ 10,500	+ 14,400	+ 0.2	+ 0.3
Lower Normandy	+ 55,500	- 14,400	- 0.6	- 0.2
Pays de la Loire	- 42,000	- 10,900	- 0.2	- 0.1
Brittany	- 67,400	- 12,500	- 0.4	- 0.1
Limousin	- 6,700	+ 6,900	- 0.1	+ 0.2
Auvergne	- 1,500	+ 20,500	- 0.0	+ 0.3
Poitou Charentes	- 26,900	- 19,000	- 0.2	- 0.2
Aquitaine	+ 44,500	+ 96,800	+ 0.3	+ 0.7
Midi Pyrénées	+ 34,400	+ 91,500	+ 0.2	+ 0.7
Burgundy	+ 15,800	+ 28,900	+ 0.1	+ 0.3
Rhône Alpes	+ 219,400	+ 224,500	+ 0.7	+ 0.9
Languedoc Roussillon	+ 76,700	+ 122,900	+ 0.7	+ 1.3
Provence Côte d'Azur	+ 343,600	+ 390,200	+ 1.7	+ 2.2
Corsica	+ 24,200	+ 9,400	+ 1.2	- 0.6

SOURCE: INSEE.

13

(in '000)

Table 3. NUMBERS EMPLOYED

REGIONS	1954 CENSUS	1962 CENSUS	1968 CENSUS	FORECASTS FOR 1.1.1976 END OF VIth PLAN
Paris Region	3,577	4,006	4,294	4,796
Champagne	476	479	508	554
Picardy	544	560	605	695
Upper Normandy	543	565	611	693
Centre	774	763	799	873
Lower Normandy	533	508	532	557
Burgundy	586	567	588	623
North	1,338	1,321	1,337	1,442
Lorraine	799	830	838	920
Alsace	546	533	560	627
France Comté	377	374	396	431
Pays de la Loire	1,058	1,012	1,044	1,101
Brittany	1,072	991	992	1,011
Poitou Charentes	587	556	570	593
Aquitaine	1,014	956	976	1,035
Midi Pyrénées	865	822	828	853
Limousin	359	319	307	304
Rhône Alpes	1,666	1,725	1,833	2,026
Auvergne	562	517	529	549
Languedoc	536	540	574	609
Provence Côte d'Azur	967	1,059	1,189	1,351
Corsica	66	76	62	70
Whole of France	18,845	19,080	19,972	21,713

SOURCE: Plan - INSEE.

14

THE 22 REGIONS

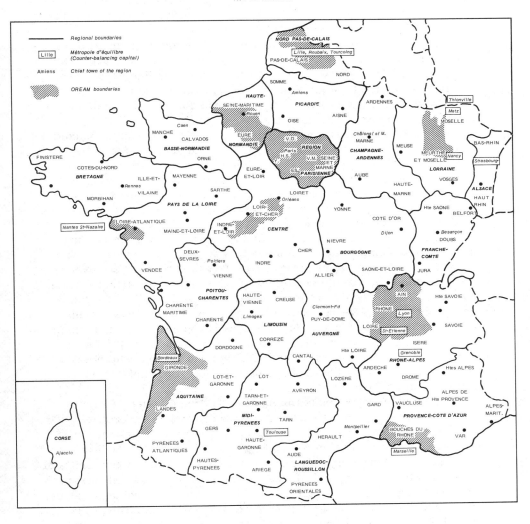

Legend:

— Regional boundaries

Lille — Métropole d'équilibre (Counter-balancing capital)

Amiens — Chief town of the region

OREAM boundaries

NORD PAS-DE-CALAIS
Lille, Roubaix, Tourcoing
PAS-DE-CALAIS
NORD
SOMME
Amiens
HAUTE-
SEINE-MARITIME
PICARDIE
Rouen
OISE
AISNE
ARDENNES
Thionville
Metz
MOSELLE
MANCHE
Caen
CALVADOS
EURE
MARNE
Châlons/s/M.
MEUSE
MEURTHE
ET MOSELLE
Nancy
BAS-RHIN
BASSE-NORMANDIE
NORMANDIE
V.O.
REGION
Paris
CHAMPAGNE-
ARDENNES
LORRAINE
Strasbourg
FINISTERE
ORNE
H.S.
V.M. SEINE
ET
MARNE
AUBE
VOSGES
ALSACE
COTES-DU-NORD
EURE-
ET-LOIR
E.S.
PARISIENNE
HAUTE-
MARNE
Hte SAONE
HAUT
RHIN
BELFORT
BRETAGNE
ILLE-ET-
VILAINE
MAYENNE
SARTHE
LOIRET
YONNE
COTE D'OR
Dijon
Besançon
DOUBS
FRANCHE-
COMTE
Rennes
MORBIHAN
LOIRE-ATLANTIQUE
Nantes St-Nazaire
MAINE-ET-LOIRE
INDRE-
ET-LOIR
LOIR-
ET-CHER
Orléans
CENTRE
NIEVRE
BOURGOGNE
JURA
PAYS DE LA LOIRE
DEUX-
SEVRES
VENDEE
Poitiers
VIENNE
INDRE
CHER
ALLIER
SAONE-ET-LOIRE
AIN
Hte SAVOIE
CHARENTE
MARITIME
POITOU-
CHARENTES
HAUTE-
VIENNE
Limoges
CREUSE
Clermont-Fd
PUY-DE-DOME
RHONE
Lyon
St-Etienne
LOIRE
SAVOIE
CHARENTE
LIMOUSIN
CORREZE
AUVERGNE
ISERE
Grenoble
Bordeaux
GIRONDE
DORDOGNE
CANTAL
Hte LOIRE
RHONE-ALPES
ARDECHE
DROME
Htes ALPES
AQUITAINE
LANDES
LOT-ET-
GARONNE
LOT
AVEYRON
LOZERE
ALPES DE
Hte PROVENCE
ALPES
MARIT.
TARN-ET-
GARONNE
GARD
VAUCLUSE
PROVENCE-COTE D'AZUR
MIDI-
PYRENEES
GERS
TARN
Montpellier
BOUCHES DU
RHONE
VAR
CORSE
Ajaccio
PYRENEES
ATLANTIQUES
Toulouse
HAUTE-
GARONNE
HERAULT
Marseille
HAUTES-
PYRENEES
ARIEGE
AUDE
LANGUEDOC-
ROUSSILLON
PYRENEES
ORIENTALES

15

The least advanced regions have progressed as fast, and sometimes faster, than the other regions. The ten regions West of the
line Le Havre/Marseille which account for 56% of the national territory
and contained only 37% of the total population and 25% of the working
population in industry at the start of the VIth Plan in 1966 lost 400,000
people during the period 1954-62 but gained 200,000 between 1962 and
1968. In Brittany migration fell by two-thirds.

Of the eight "metropoles d'équilibre" (counter-balancing capitals):
Lille, Roubaix-Tourcoing, Nancy-Metz-Thionville, Strasbourg, Saint
Etienne-Grenoble, Marseille, Toulouse, Bordeaux, Nantes-Saint-
Nazaire all but the first grew more quickly than the capital.

Provincial urban centres with more than 200,000 inhabitants grew
up by 15% compared with 8% in the case of Paris.

It remains the case that the growth of Paris continued to be considerable, total population rising by 770,000 from 1962 to 1968. Its
present annual average rate of growth has fallen to 1.4% compared
with 1.7% between 1954 and 1962. Though it still attracts migratory
movements the number of people to leave the Paris region for other
regions was between 1952-1968 almost as great as the number arriving
in Paris from the Provinces.

As has been indicated in the "Re-appraisal" changes in regional
population and employment and migratory flows often represent the
normal processes of adjustment of a society to changes in the underlying economic and social conditions which are a hall-mark of a dynamic
society. They may also reflect the influence of the deliberate policies
designed to modify the regional balance that would otherwise result
from conditions of change. Such policies have been adopted in France
in the successive 5 years Plans and incorporate the concept of area
redevelopment (aménagement du territoire) and will have been a
contributory factor to the changing distribution of population and
employment described above.

It should of course be borne in mind that the division of France
into 22 programme regions may tend to exaggerate the importance of
interregional movement. Such a number of regions mean that the
regions are relatively small (compared for example with the 8 regions
of England) and interregional movement may represent in part shifts of
population over fairly small distances rather than major redistribution
for some large sections of the country to others. For some purposes
of comparison particularly in relation to regional disparities, it is
useful to adopt a smaller number of larger areas, the Zones d'étude
et d'Aménagement du Territoire (see Statistiques et Indicateurs des
Régions Françaises, Edition 1972).

Of significance as an indicator of regional disparities is the
variation in activity rates (active population as a proportion of total)
in the eight study regions in 1971, i.e.

STUDY REGIONS	ACTIVE POPULATION (%)		
	M. AND F.	M.	F.
Paris Region	48.1	58.8	38.3
Paris Bassin	40.8	53.1	29.0
North	36.2	48.9	24.0
East	38.8	52.3	25.9
West	40.4	52.1	29.6
South West	40.7	53.3	29.0
Centre East	41.6	55.0	29.0
Mediterranean	38.1	52.4	25.0
Totality	41.4	53.8	29.8

The table shows the considerable disparity between the Paris region and the rest of the country and the particularly low place of the North, East and Mediterranean zones. It also shows a correspondingly low level, in these zones, of female employment.

Average gross per capita incomes provides a further indicator of regional disparities. For 1968 the average in the Paris region was 139% of the national average. Of the other regions only Alsace reached the national average, the remainder varying from 81% (Brittany) to 98% (Rhone-Alpes).

Thus, in addition to the factor of regional unevenness in change and growth there is also the factor of regional disparities, (of which other indicators besides activity rates and revenues would need to be given to provide a full picture of the regional structure).

Certain types of problems arise out of the changes in regional structure and the disparities which have been briefly described.

i) In the areas and regions most directly affected by the run down of employment in the basic industries, of agriculture and mining, the problem of securing alternative employment, of a satisfactory kind, for the displaced or for the rising generation who would, in earlier times have been employed in these industries. Alternative employment would need to be on a scale sufficient to avoid an unacceptable level of out-migration.

ii) The growth of population, interregional shifts and increasing urbanisation tends to focus on certain areas, zones, or urban centres, rather than others, creating the problems of the adaptation of those areas, in infrastructure, housing and social equipment to enable them to cope with the problems of expansion.

iii)   Insofar as certain areas of attraction cannot absorb the in-coming population without leading to unacceptable levels of congestion, overcrowding, as well as to inflationary pressures in the work force, the problem of finding alternative areas of attraction which can be developed without such difficulties.   The most notable problem in this field is of course providing alternatives to the further expansion of the capital.

iv)   To the extent that unacceptable disparities exist between regions, in income levels, standards of living, social welfare and "quality of life" the problem of ensuring that the development of the economy or its growth takes place in a way which will enable such disparities to be lessened or eradicated.

C.   THE DEVELOPMENT OF THE APPROACH TO REGIONAL POLICIES

In France regional policies have constituted an integral part of national policies as expressed in the successive 5 year Plans.   The basic framework was provided in 1954 by the division of France into "regional action areas", subsequently called Programme Regions, numbering (with the addition of Corsica in 1972) 22.

During these two decades regional policy has evolved both as circumstances changed and trends became more clearly defined.   In the more recent period of the Vth and VIth Plans four factors conditioned the approach to regional policy:

a)   the increasing importance attached to international development and, in particular, conditions of competition in Europe;

b)   the failure of the earlier policies marked by the continued predominance of Paris, the insufficiently qualitative development of the West and the minor role of some "métropoles d'équilibre" ;

c)   the emergence of new phenomena such as the importance of the tertiary sector in creating new jobs and the difficulties encountered in the development of regions in the East and North (Alsace, Lorraine, North).   Many are having to contend with more vigorous growth on their borders ;

d)   the new emphasis placed by the population on the environment, leading to greater opposition to geographical mobility and a calling into question of industrialisation and urbanisation and a demand for improve-ment in living conditions ("quality of life") rather than the standard of living as such.

These basic conditions present a complex range of interconnected problems, in terms of economic, physical planning and social develop-ment.   It is in recognition of this that regional policy in France has evolved, within a framework of national (indicative) planning into a comprehensive policy of area development (aménagement du territoire) extending to France as a whole. Three general aims - ultimate objectives in the sense this term is used in the "Re-appraisal" - can be said to underly current area redevelopment policy:

i) ensuring the more rational use of productive capacity, in particular by incorporating the long term factor in the calculations of entrepreneurs and administrations - a forward looking or anticipatory role in economic development ;

ii) achieving "balanced" development, both between the various regions and within each region, and between town and country - a corrective role;

iii) the improvement of people's living conditions in such a way as to safeguard the natural environment and ensure that everybody, whatever his place of birth or domicile, has the best possible opportunities with regard to training and advancement - the social role.

The strategic targets implied in these broad aims are fivefold:

one - establishing a better balance between Paris and the provinces. This involves curbing the population and industrial growth of the Paris region, decentralising economic activity away from Paris, to the Paris Basin and beyond, and developing new jobs (estimated at 250,000 in the VIth Plan) in industry in the provinces. At the same time emphasis is placed on improving the productivity of enterprises in Paris and, above all, on its role as an international capital;

two - developing the West (8 regions) as a priority to increase the ratio of industrial and tertiary sector jobs (from 75% in 1968 to 80% by 1975);

three - improving the situation of the border areas in the North and East to offset the decline of mining, iron and steel and textile industries and the pull of the neighbouring German and Swiss regions (with more dynamic industries and higher salaries);

four - improving the densely populated and most highly developed areas in regard to general facilities and living conditions;

five - development of the rural areas by modernisation of agriculture, extension of secondary industry, tourism and tertiary sector activities generally and by nature conservation. The regions most concerned are primarily those that are losing their farming populations: the West, Massif Central and South West as well as the mountain communes.

Such major aims and targets involve negative and positive measures - negative to restrain the growth of Paris and positive, to encourage the establishment of suitable secondary and tertiary industries in the preferred regional locations, including the metropoles d'équilibre or

regional capitals, and to provide the necessary physical and social
infrastructure - communications, housing, education and health
facilities required in the areas of conversion or expansion.

D. THE INSTRUMENTS OF REGIONAL POLICIES

Three main instruments, or types of measures are used in France
to secure the objectives described above:

a) Measures to guide employment to preferred locations or loca-
    localities;
b) Urban and towns policy;
c) The orientation of infrastructural investment policy.

a) Employment guidance

Both negative and positive measures are used to curb growth within
the Paris region. The creation or the extension of an industrial enterprise exceeding a total net floor area of 1,500 square metres, and of
office premises exceeding 1,000 square metres require administrative
authorisation and is subject to a tax, the amount of which varies according to the proximity to the centre of the capital, the further away
the lower the tax. The amount of the tax varies between Frs 25 and
Frs 150 per square metre of the floor area for industrial premises and
Frs 100 and Frs 400 per square metre of office premises.

As a positive measure industries in the Paris region and the five
cantons in the Oise Department which transfer all or part of their plant
to the provinces receive a decentralisation allowance equal to 60% of
removal costs provided they vacate at least 500 square metres of floor
area.

These regulations designed to curb the growth of the Paris region
are coupled with an incentive arrangement mainly consisting of awarding
an investment subsidy in the form of a development grant to entreprises
setting up in, or moving to the least developed areas.

This system was introduced in 1955 but both its geographical application and the subsidy rates and their conditions of allocation have been
modified several times since. It was first applied to industrial activities
before being extended to tertiary activities in 1972.

It should be noted that the negative measures do not constitute a ban
of development in the Paris region. A firm that is willing to pay the
tax remains free to locate or expand in the region. Administrative
authorisation is generally given on condition that a firm undertakes
part of its investment in the provinces. The control system is used
as much to distribute industrial and tertiary activities within the Paris
region as to facilitate the decentralisation policy. It is administered
flexibly and greater reliance is placed on assistance to encourage
location elsewhere, the final decision being left to the enterprise.

The positive measures consist of a variety of forms of financial and other assistance, varying between the different areas of France.

At present (1974) the regional development grant can be awarded to industrial enterprises and, occasionally, to new or expanding tertiary enterprises. In the first case they have to increase their staff by either at least 30% or 100 people.

The system is adjusted according to the site area (see map).

Normal rates are as follows:

12% of investment in buildings and equipment and applies to most regions in the West, some in the East (particularly the Vosges), Corsica.

12% (extensions), 15% (new establishments) Brittany and Atlantic Pyrénées.

20% (extensions), 25% (new establishments). In fourteen urban centres in the West, in the border areas in the North and East and various mining areas in the Centre.

The maximum rate of grant is Frs. 15,000 per new job for new enterprises and Frs. 12,000 for extensions. This aid system is more flexible in rural modernisation areas and Corsica with regard both to the conditions of job creation and the minimum amount of investments required.

The areas which receive regional development grants, the metropoles d'équilibre and nine other towns (Besançon, Dijon, Grenoble, Clermont-Ferrand, Aix, Nice, Cannes, Montpellier, Caen) can qualify for grants for attracting tertiary activities on condition that the investment programmes result in the creation of at least 100 permanent jobs (50 in the case of research departments).

In 1972 the total value of the grants awarded by the Government amounted to some Frs. 370 millions (equivalent to some 25,000 jobs.)

Other forms of assistance include loans from public funds at reduced rates (about 2 points below market rates, two year exemption from local registration tax (patente), higher depreciation allowance on buildings (25% in the first year as compared with 5% normally) labour force training and retraining assistance, reductions in the price of land and various types of aid from local authorities and bodies.

In total the cost of all the aid taken together has varied over recent years between 200 and 500 million frs. This may be regarded as comparatively small in relation to the scale of the problem of regional development. It compares with 6,000 million frs. per annum in agricultural market support and 2,000 million frs in support of the coal industry (though in a sense these also represent assistance to the regions).

The limitations on the total value of the assistance reflect a number of features. The system is selective, in that the kind of assistance granted in each case is discretionary and subject to negotiation, often prolonged; loans are given only in exceptional circumstances; local authority assistance is discretionary; and it is both conditional on job creation and subject to maxima per job created.

b) Urban towns policy

Urban and town policy is a vital element in French regional policy. It is necessitated not only by the tendency to migration from rural areas to the towns, a factor common to most advanced countries, but also from the increasing urbanisation of a growing population. In addition, the problem of slowing the relative growth of Paris imposes the necessity of providing alternative urban centres capable of fulfilling, in part at least, some of the functions which have been almost wholly centralised in the capital. Moreover, in France as elsewhere the structure and facilities - in housing, transport and social equipment - in many of the older towns is inadequate to meet satisfactorily the needs of the expanding populations. Both industrialisation and the growth of the tertiary sector also require the adaptation of existing centres and the development of new urban areas to provide land space for the factories, offices, housing, hospitals and schools which are a concomitant of economic growth.

Thus the area redevelopment policy on the urban plane comprises several elements. First, the adaptation of Paris itself to the continued growth which, so far, and despite regional policy, has proved inescapable. This entails especially the provision of additional areas for housing, up to a ceiling of 500,000 units within the VIth Plan and a further 100,000 units in five new towns in the region.

Second, the designation of existing major towns or collections of towns as "métropoles d'équilibre", capable of providing, in each region, a "capital" or focal point of urban development in which new industrial and tertiary development can occur on a significant scale by development and utilisation of an already existing infrastructure. This gives rise to a number of priorities with regard to decentralisation (the aero-space industry in Toulouse) and improvements in communications. It involves also the preparation and implementation of suitable redevelopment places for the metropoles d'équilibre, and the provincial new towns in their neighbourhoods to restore balanced growth of the urban complexes: l'Isle d'Abeau near Lyon; Lille-Est; Le Vaudreuil near Rouen; l'Etang de Berre near Marseille. Each has been given a degree of priority and individual budget treatment under the VIth Plan.

Urban development policy also includes giving attention to the medium sized towns (which between 1962 and 1968 grew in population as much as the 20 towns with more than 200,000 inhabitants) by placing new means at their disposal (maximum rate of development grant and special aid to infrastructure). New centres for heavy industry, requiring maritime seabord locations have also been established at Fos (near Marseille) and Dunkirk in the North.

REGIONAL DEVELOPMENT GRANT

normal rate - 12%   increased rate 12%, expansion 15%, new investments   maximum rate 20%, expansion 25%, new investments   areas with predominantly agricultural economies

PAS-DE-CALAIS
Lille
Arras
NORD
Amiens
SOMME
Charleville-Mézières
SEINE-MARITIME
OISE
AISNE
ARDENNES
Rouen
Beauvais
Laon
MANCHE
MEUSE
Metz
MOSELLE
BAS-RHIN
Caen
CALVADOS
EURE
REGION
MARNE
Chalons-s-Marne
Bar-Le-Duc
Nancy
MEURTHE-ET-MOSELLE
Strasbourg
St-Lo
Evreux
Paris
PARISIENNE
FINISTERE
ORNE
EURE-ET-LOIR
AUBE
Colmar
HAUT-RHIN
Epinal
VOSGES
St-Brieuc
Alençon
Chartres
Troyes
Chaumont
HAUTE-SAONE
Quimper
COTES-DU-NORD
MAYENNE
Le Mans
LOIR-ET-CHER
LOIRET
Orléans
HAUTE-MARNE
Vesoul
DOUBS
TERRITOIRE DE BELFORT
ILLE-ET-VILAINE
Rennes
Laval
SARTHE
Auxerre
YONNE
COTE-D'OR
Besançon
MORBIHAN
Vannes
LOIRE-ATLANTIQUE
Angers
MAINE-ET-LOIRE
Tours
INDRE-ET-LOIRE
Blois
Bourges
NIEVRE
Dijon
SAONE-ET-LOIRE
JURA
Lons-Le-Saunier
Nantes
VENDEE
DEUX-SEVRES
VIENNE
Poitiers
INDRE
Chateauroux
CHER
Nevers
Moulins
La Roche-s-Yon
Niort
ALLIER
Macon
Bourg
AIN
HAUTE-SAVOIE
Annecy
La Rochelle
CHARENTE-MARITIME
CHARENTE
HAUTE-VIENNE
Guéret
CREUSE
PUY-DE-DOME
Lyon
RHONE
St-Etienne
LOIRE
Chambéry
SAVOIE
Angoulême
Limoges
Clermont-Ferrand
ISERE
Grenoble
Périgueux
CORREZE
Tulle
CANTAL
HTE-LOIRE
Le Puy
ARDECHE
Valence
Htes-ALPES
Bordeaux
DORDOGNE
Aurillac
Privas
DROME
Gap
GIRONDE
LOT
AVEYRON
LOZERE
Mende
ALPES
Digne
ALPES-Mmes
Cahors
LOT-ET-GARONNE
Rodez
GARD
VAUCLUSE
DE Hte-PROVENCE
Nice
LANDES
Agen
TARN-ET-GARONNE
Montauban
TARN
Albi
Montpellier
HERAULT
Nimes
Avignon
VAR
Draguignan
Mont-de-Marsan
GERS
Auch
HTE-GARONNE
Toulouse
Carcassonne
Bches DU RHONE
Marseille
PYRENEES-ATLANTIQUES
Pau
Tarbes
HAUTES PYRENEES
ARIEGE
Foix
AUDE
Perpignan
PYR. ORIENTALES
CORSE
Ajaccio

23

Finally, communes which set up Urban Communities can benefit by entering into Plan Contracts with the Government covering three year capital expenditure and even operating expenditure

Thus urban development policy can be regarded as an integral part of general regional policy, designed to encourage economic development in selected areas and to provide for social needs throughout the country under the pressures of increasing urbanisation.

c) Infrastructure development

Neither assistance to industry, nor the formulation of an urban development policy can be successful without appropriate investment in the infrastructure. Urban development involves changes in space use, with attendant problems of, inter alia, communications and transport. In rural areas and towns alike the expansion of economic activity requires, in addition to suitable labour, the provision of infrastructure in all forms.

The infrastructure requirements of regional policy are met in two main ways. First, by Inter-Ministerial coordination, regarded as the best way to ensure that investments by the various Ministries are consistent with the aims of area redevelopment. Second, the use of special funds, the F.I.A.T. (Fonds d'Investissement d'Aménagement du Territoire) and (since 1972) the F.A.D. (Fonds d'Aide à la Décentralisation) to supplement the normal budget appropriations of the various Ministries to launch or accelerate capital expenditure or to facilitate establishment of activities in the provinces. In addition special funds exist for allocation to Rural Renovation Areas (Brittany, Manche, Limousin, Lot, Auvergne, mountain areas.)

Inter-ministerial coordination under the Plan is however by far the more important of the two methods, since this determines how far regional considerations will govern the allocation of the bulk of Government expenditure in infrastructure. The special funds provide in total around 1,000 million frs. each year, one half of one percent of a total Government budget of the order of 200 billion frs. and one tenth of one percent of a GDP of frs. 1,000 billion.

E. DEVELOPMENT OF METHODOLOGY

French regional policy, as it has evolved, is marked by a number of distinctive features in the field of methodology which warrant the assertion that France is among the leading exponents, or even the leading exponent, of a methodological approach which can be described as both comprehensive and systematic.

The comprehensive nature of the French regional policy is evidenced firstly by its nation-wide coverage. A basic framework is provided by the division of the whole of France since 1954 into regional action areas, and subsequently into the 22 programme regions. Secondly, the requirements of regional policy are integrated into the national plans. Thirdly, regional policy is not confined to one aspect but seeks to deal with all aspects of development, economic, urban development, infrastructure, social facilities, in accordance with the strategic objectives of national planning.

Basic to any comprehensive approach is the provision, appraisal and evaluation of data and information, and the development of research into economic and social trends. Marked progress has been made in this field, exemplified by the comprehensive regional statistics produced annually by the National Institute of Statistics and Economic Studies, the studies and reports of the National Area Redevelopment Commission (Commission Nationale à l'Aménagement du Territoire) the DATAR (Délégation à l'Aménagement du Territoire et à l'Action Régionale) and, at regional level, of the studies by regional and local administrative bodies and by the ORGAM (Regional Organisations for the Study of Metropolitan Areas).

Considerable attention has also been paid to organisational questions, to provide adequate administrative machinery to carry out the tasks of coordination, preparation and implementation of plans and programmes. At the central level the Commissariat Général du Plan is entrusted with guiding the work of the Commission Nationale à l'Aménagement du Territoire and is responsible for the regionalisation of the Plan, while the DATAR is entrusted with the task of interministerial co-ordination in the light of the regionalisation of the Budget. Its regional policy action is illustrated by the preparation and implementation of the whole system of aid for the decentralisation, conversion and development of industrial and tertiary activities throughout the country as well as responsibility for promoting policies concerning the metropoles d'équilibre and major industrial areas of national importance such as Fos. The Commission à l'Aménagement du Territoire provides reports on guide-lines for the National Plan for consideration as well as outline plans for major infrastructure programmes which can affect the balance between regions.

At the regional level the administrative bodies set up in 1964 introduced regional Prefects, assisted by regional missions, and a Consultative Commission (CODER) as well as representation of actual Government Departments at the level of Departments and Regions. In recent years emphasis has also been placed on regional decentralisation of central Government aimed at placing more responsibility for programming measures in the hands of regional administrative Departments and to encourage closer cooperation between Central Government at regional level and local authorities and socio-economic bodies. This process is by no means completed but increasingly it should bring about a greater coordination between the national and regional components of area redevelopment or regional policy as a whole.

At the political level, further measures designed to increase regional participation in regional policy formulation have been under consideration.

Among other features of methodology are to be noted the graduation of financial incentives, i.e. the differential scales applying to different areas and as between the industrial and tertiary sectors, and the existence of special funds (FIAT and FAD and Rural Renovation Appropriations) to supplement the normal capital expenditures on infrastructure. While they play some part in encouraging desirable development from a regional policy point of view, they are small in total. It is therefore a significant feature of the methodology of regional policy that much greater reliance is placed on influencing the direction of national investment policy as a whole towards those objectives of regional policy that are incorporated in the National Plan.

F. CONCLUSIONS DRAWN FROM EXPERIENCE

French regional policies, which have now, with modifications been in operation for two decades have had both successes and failures and it is possible to discern some of the strengths and weaknesses.

As regards inter-regional balance of employment, the number of jobs in industry in the Paris region has fallen by almost 5% since 1962 whereas between 1954 and 1962 a third of all jobs created in industry were in this region.

By contrast, 700,000 new jobs in industry have been created in the Provinces since 1954 and the rate of creation has tended to accelerate rising from 22,000 per annum between 1954 and 1962 to 60,000 between 1968 and 1972.

The 8 regions of the West of France were the main beneficiaries, overall industrial employment having risen by 25% in the ten years to 1971. In the conversion, mining, iron and steel, areas some 80,000 new jobs have been created since 1968. In the areas with predominantly agricultural economies rural migration has been partially checked and the desertion or abandonment of the countryside particularly in the hinterland of Britanny and in mountain areas has been prevented.

On the other hand problems remain in the conversion areas, particularly in the North and Lorraine which are handicapped by obsolete equipment and facilities and by the strong foreign competition on their doorstep. Moreover, recent studies have shown that regional disparities in incomes have not been significantly reduced.

Weaknesses in the implementation of the Vth and VIth Plans are indicated by the fact that the final distribution of capital expenditure was hardly in conformity with the expressed area redevelopment orientations. The regions that have benefitted the most were those containing the métropoles d'équilibre and were also given the majority of major projects, particularly for motorways.

The positive changes in favour of decentralisation of industrial employment of the Paris region and some conversion areas cannot be wholly attributed to the policies pursued. The effectiveness of industrial aids is, as has been noted above, limited. It is possible that much decentralisation would have taken place in any case, since circumstances have encouraged enterprises to create many jobs requiring few occupational skills in regions where wages are lower (eg. in the West) thereby exploiting sources of labour without setting up sub-contracting networks and without becoming sufficiently part of the local economy to ensure that the region can develop independently.

The most significant weakness, or indeed failure in regional policy results however from the insufficient attention given to the regional implications of the growth of the tertiary sector. This bears particularly on the problem of decentralisation of the Paris region. Only very few enterprises have been willing to decentralise and the creation of tertiary sector jobs in the provinces remains inadequate from both the qualitative and quantitative standpoints.

Thus, between 1967 and 1971 the proportion of office space authorised in the Paris region was increasing to such an extent that at present more than half the office space created in France is in this region. The seriousness of this situation is likely to be aggravated by the fact that the tertiary sector is now the most rapidly expanding sector of the French economy. While the VIth Plan provided for the creation of 250,000 jobs in industry it allowed for a growth of 750,000 tertiary sector jobs. Thus much depends on how far regional policy can influence the location of those jobs outside the Paris region.

It would seem to be a fair conclusion that the regional structure of France has changed in recent decades, not so much because of the influence of regional policies but because of those factors which have brought about the expansion of its economy, eg. the growth of population and work force, the expansion of new industrial sectors and of tertiary industries and the large extension in the in the infrastructure. Development has therefore tended to occur as much in the traditionally developed regions and urban areas as elsewhere.

While France has developed a policy and an organisation which permits efforts to influence the development of the weak regions, the appearance of new problems, especially in the frontier regions, and the need for the development of infrastructure, especially for transportation in the most competitive regions, has not enabled the concentration of collective investment efforts in the Western regions. These regions have, however, witnessed an economic renewal underlined by the re-establishment of the migration balance. It is true that they are developing less rapidly than the densely populated regions but their resources in manpower and land space constitute a considerable asset which, if it is reinforced with a policy for the improvement of communications, should enable a re-establishment of the regional balance in favour of those regions.

G. EXPECTATIONS

The future course of the French economy is, as elsewhere, clouded by uncertainty. The main trends which affect regional balance are still in operation, particularly the decline in agricultural employment and the influence of international competition while the expansion in the tertiary sector may continue to favour the development of the Paris region. It is difficult, however, to foresee that the overt objectives of regional policy will become less important in the future. On the contrary, the need would seem to be to go further on the path already charted, to increase the effectiveness and impact of the measures adopted to secure a better distribution of incomes and opportunities for the people in all regions. Bearing in mind that the support given to certain sectors of the economy, notably agriculture and coal mining, by far outweigh that given to regional redevelopment, it would seem possible that a strengthened regional policy may provide an alternative to a policy of support of declining sectors, in a way which will ensure the more balanced regional growth of the French economy as a whole. It is encouraging that the machinery exists for devising suitable strategies, at national and regional levels. Given the will, the prospects of securing a satisfactory regional structure must be deemed favourable.

II

ITALY

A. THE NATIONAL PERSPECTIVE

In 1951, following the initial post-war years, the total population of
Italy stood at 47. 1 million. By 1967 it had risen to 53. 5 million and by
1972 to 54.3 million, the annual rate of increase in the decade to 1972
averaging 0. 67%, reflecting a relatively high natural growth rate (the
highest, except for the Netherlands and Ireland, in the EEC) and
moderated by persistent and high net outward migration (totalling over
500,000 in the decade 1960-1969) of which some 42% goes to other
Member countries of the Community. For the majority of emigrants
this represents a permanent rather than temporary uprooting. The
active population (civilian employment) did not rise correspondingly.
Owing to age structure and to emigration, largely of people of working
age, the total numbers in civil employment fluctuated, rising to a
maximum of 20 million in 1958-1962 and falling thereafter to 18. 7 million in 1966 and, with further fluctuations, reaching 18. 1 million in
1972. The male active population remained however more or less
static, the net decline being almost wholly attributable to a decline in
female employment.

The period from 1951 saw a massive and rapid expansion in the
national economy. Between 1951 and 1967 GDP more than doubled,
rising from 15. 4 thousand billion lire to 36 thousand billion lire in
1967 (1963 prices). In the same period gross investment virtually
trebled, rising from 2. 5 thousand billion lire to 7. 5 thousand billion
lire in 1967. Gross income (at 1963 prices) increased at an average
annual rate of 5.3% in 1951-58, 6. 6% from 1958-63, falling however
to 4. 1% in 1963-66 and rising to 6% in 1966-70. Over the period 1951
to 1970 as a whole the rate averaged 5. 6%. Subsequently there has
been a slackening: 1. 6% increase in 1971 and 3. 2% increase in 1972.
Table 1 shows the variations in gross national product since 1951.

In structural terms the overall growth of the economy was characterised by the decline in the relative importance of agriculture and the
expansion of manufacturing industry and the tertiary sectors. While
the value of output rose in all sectors the rate of increase was far
greater in those outside agriculture. Thus between 1951 and 1967
the gross product (of the private sector at factor cost, 1963 prices)

rose in agriculture from 2.9 thousand billion lire to 4.2, or 44%. Industry however increased from 4.1 to 13.3 thousand billion lire, or 217%, while tertiary activities increased from 4.9 thousand billion to 10.7, a rise of 119%. In employment terms the shift was even more marked, agricultural employment declining by 4 million between 1951-66, while industrial employment rose by nearly 2 million, tertiary activities by about 1 million and general Government by half a million. In 1951 agriculture accounted for 44% of total employment. By 1966 the proportion had fallen to 24.3% and by 1972 to 18.2%, whereas in industry the proportion rose from 29.4% in 1951 to 39.8% in 1966 and to 44.3% in 1972.

While the period up to 1963 was marked by continuing high growth rates, the subsequent period saw set backs and fluctuations. The expansion of the economy reflected not only domestic features but the increasing role of international trade, especially within the EEC as a major contributor to the growth of export industries and domestic consumption.

Both underemployment (particularly in the South) and unemployment have constituted serious problems but have changed over time. Total unemployment fell from 1.5 million in 1957 (6.9% of the labour force) to 504 thousand in 1963 (2.5%), rose in subsequent years to 769 thousand in 1966 (3.4%) but by 1971 had fallen to 281 thousand. In October 1974 unemployment reached 605 thousand (3.1%) to which should be added 314 thousand on reduced working hours giving a total of 919 thousand (4.5%). However, these figures are purely indicative and only give some idea of the scale of the phenomenon. In the first place there are statistical difficulties involved and it is the upward trend which is disquieting; 738 thousand in April 1974 to 919 thousand in October 1974. Secondly, the data are global and do not reflect the true situation in the South where about half of the unemployment occurs although approximately one third of the active population is in the South.

Thus, while the main feature of the Italian economy in the post-war years has been its rapid and large expansion and industrialisation, accompanied by advances in technology and productivity, the picture is not an unmixed one. The average level of incomes has remained below that of the majority of European countries, while fluctuations in the economy, the prevalence of underemployment and, at times, high unemployment, masked to some degree by high emigration especially to other European countries, indicate that the growth of the economy has not reached the limits of the possibilities it would have if sufficient investment resources were available and its labour resources were fully utilised.

B. THE EMERGENCE OF REGIONAL PROBLEMS AND THEIR NATURE

The characteristic regional problem of Italy is, as is well known, the "dualism" of the Italian economy, the contrast between North and

Table 1.   AVERAGE ANNUAL RATES OF VARIATION IN GROSS NATIONAL PRODUCT AT MARKET PRICES

(in 1963 prices)

FINAL YEAR / INITIAL YEAR	1952	1953	1954	1955	1956	1957	1958	1959	1960	1961	1962	1963	1964 [1]	1965	1966	1967	1968	1969	1970	1971	1972
1951	4.5	6.0	5.2	5.6	5.4	5.4	5.3	5.5	5.6	5.8	5.9	5.8	5.6	5.5	5.5	5.6	5.6	5.6	5.6	5.4	5.3
1952		7.5	5.6	5.9	5.6	5.6	5.5	5.6	5.7	6.0	6.0	6.0	5.7	5.6	5.6	5.7	5.7	5.7	5.7	5.4	5.3
1953			3.6	5.1	5.0	5.1	5.1	5.3	5.5	5.8	5.9	5.8	5.5	5.4	5.4	5.5	5.6	5.6	5.6	5.3	5.2
1954				6.7	5.7	5.6	5.4	5.7	5.8	6.1	6.2	6.1	5.7	5.6	5.6	5.7	5.7	5.7	5.7	5.4	5.3
1955					4.8	5.1	5.0	5.4	5.6	6.0	6.1	6.0	5.6	5.4	5.5	5.6	5.6	5.7	5.6	5.3	5.2
1956						5.4	5.1	5.6	5.8	6.3	6.3	6.2	5.8	5.5	5.6	5.7	5.7	5.7	5.7	5.4	5.2
1957							4.9	5.8	5.9	6.5	6.5	6.3	5.8	5.5	5.7	5.7	5.8	5.8	5.7	5.4	5.3
1958								6.6	6.5	7.1	6.9	6.6	6.0	5.6	5.7	5.7	5.8	5.8	5.8	5.4	5.3
1959									6.3	7.3	7.0	6.6	5.8	5.5	5.5	5.7	5.7	5.7	5.7	5.3	5.2
1960										8.3	7.3	6.7	5.7	5.3	5.4	5.6	5.7	5.7	5.6	5.2	5.1
1961											6.3	5.8	4.8	4.5	4.8	5.2	5.3	5.4	5.3	4.9	4.8
1962												5.4	4.1	4.0	4.5	4.9	5.1	5.2	5.2	4.8	4.6
1963													2.9	3.3	4.1	4.8	5.1	5.2	5.2	4.7	4.6
1964														3.6	4.8	5.5	5.7	5.7	5.6	5.0	4.2
1965															5.9	6.4	6.4	6.2	5.9	5.2	4.9
1966																6.8	6.6	6.3	6.0	5.1	4.8
1967																	6.4	6.1	5.7	4.6	4.3
1968																		5.7	5.1	4.1	3.8
1969																			4.9	3.2	3.2
1970																				1.6	2.4
1971																					3.2

South, of a kind and degree which has no parallel elsewhere in Europe. This dualism does not arise out of the recent trends noted in the preceding section but is of long standing origin. It has been a feature of the Italian State since unification over a century ago. Its causes are to be found in the comparatively unfavourable factors of physical geography, in social structure and traditions, lack of resources other than land, while unification itself favoured the industrial and commercial development of the North. For decades economic conditions and social structure permitted little more than low level subsistence farming, the difficulties of which were enhanced by inadequate water supply, erosion and the persistence of malaria in low lying coastal land, causing concentration of populations in the higher inland and mountainous areas unfavourable to a high yield agricultural economy. The legacy of these conditions was not only a low standard of living for a rapidly growing population but a general condition of backwardness, in skills, education and commercial activity and enterprise. The normal conditions for economic growth, savings and capital accumulation, enterprise, roads, water supplies and infrastructure generally were lacking. For millions, the only solution was emigration - between 1885 and 1915 some 3.5 million left the South, predominantly for the Americas.

The between-wars period saw no improvement. Investment and economic development took place mainly in the North while restrictions on migration* further increased the population almost wholly engaged in subsistence agriculture within poor and deteriorating land. The second world war brought destruction and disruption, particularly in the South and Central Italy while the industries of the North remained to provide the springboard for Italy's post-war industrial recovery and growth.

At the beginning of the post-war period three distinct major regional situations could be discerned. The three North Western regions of Piedmont, Lombardy and Liguria, with intensive industrial concentration and efficient production in all fields, gave high income with a considerable level of capital export; a second area-running from Veneto to Roma - with lower incomes, notably from manufacture, but with a healthy agriculture and a degree of balance between population and resources and well placed for economic growth; the South and the islands, with extremely low income levels, imbalance between population (38% of the total) and resources, poor agriculture and virtually no industry and deficient infrastructures and social capital. The area as a whole was characterised by a continuous worsening of the depression, inherited from the past, and was incapable of any self propulsive economic progress.

Recognition that this was an unacceptable situation has been deeply embedded in the Italian national consciousness, gaining in strength

---

* Restrictions imposed by the fascist Government in order to put a brake on the rural exodus and urbanisation of the population. These restrictions are no longer applied.

from the early post war years and continuing into the present. In absolute terms the degree of poverty and backwardness of the South went beyond tolerable limits for a modern society, while the contrast with the rest of the country could not be reconciled with social and national equity. The years from 1947 to 1953 saw therefore the foundations of national policies designed to correct what was seen as a fundamental imbalance in the national economic and social structure. The emphasis given to this aspect of national policy has itself been a formative influence on the evolution of the national economy. Italy can be said to be a locus classicus of a regional policy designed to affect the basic structure of a country rather than to modify or palliate the regional effects of economic change.

It should however be noted that the regional problems of Italy are not confined to the imbalance between North and South. Though this constitutes the major problem for policy, certain areas, in both North and Central Italy, suffer from disadvantages which limit their economic potential and give them the characteristics of depressed areas (high emigration, low industrialisation, low incomes, inefficient agriculture, etc.). In addition to mountain zones, such areas have been variously classified and defined to cover (under 1966 legislation) 24.4% of the total area of central and northern Italy and 13.6% of their populations. In recent years, questions relating to development policy in the underdeveloped and mountainous regions in the Centre North have been the subject of new legislative and administrative measures. In particular, the regional authorities concerned were given responsibility for these issues from 1971 onwards.

Moreover, the changes in the structure of the Italian economy, the relative growth of the industrial and tertiary sectors, the rural exodus and inter-regional migration led, as elsewhere, to a greater urbanisation of the country concentrating more especially in the major industrial and commercial centres and administrative centres, notably Milan, Turin, Genoa and Rome, and their surrounding areas, bringing with them the attendant problems of housing shortages, over-crowding, congestion, pollution and other social and environmental problems.

Evolution of the North/South Imbalance

A number of statistical series prepared by the Italian National Institute of Statistics in respect of Italy as a whole and broken down into four groups of regions* enable the broad evolution of the regional

---

* * The regional groupings used for purposes of statistical analysis are as follows:
   I. North-West (Piedmont, Valle d'Aosta, Lombardy, Liguria): 57.9 th. km^2 (19% of total area).
   II. North-East (Trentino - Alto Adige, Venezia, Friuli-Venezia, Giulia, Emilia - Romagna): 62th km2 (20.6%).
   III. Centre (Tuscany, Umbria, Marches, Latium): 58.3th km2 (19.3%).
   IV. South and islands (Abruzzi and Molisi, Compania, Apulia, Basilicata, Calabria, Sicily, Sardinia): 123.0th km2 (41.1%).

situation since 1951 to be seen with clarity.   The regions in groups
and individually are shown on the Map.

Population

The resident population changed between 1951 and 1971 as follows:

| REGIONS | 1951 mns | % | 1971 mns | % | CHANGE 1971/51 | |
					% +	mns
N.W.	11.7	24.8	14.9	27.6	27.7	3.2
N.E.	9.1	19.3	10.0	18.3	9.8	0.9
Centre	8.7	18.4	10.3	18.4	18.8	1.6
South	17.7	37.5	18.8	34.7	6.3	1.1
	47.1	100.0	54.0	100.0	14.6	6.9

Of the total growth of approximately 7 million nearly half was in
the North West and about one-fifth in the Centre, the growth rate in
the North/West being four and a half times and in the Centre three times
that of the South.

Implicit in these figures is the heavy migration from the South.   In
the four years 1967-70 the net balance from the South, in thousands,
was:

1967	....	120
1968	....	147
1969	....	146
1970	....	149

By contrast, in the North West the net inward balance was:

1967	....	93
1968	....	107
1969	....	106
1970	....	106

smaller increases being registered in the other two regional groups.

While, in recent years, emigration from the South was higher
than in the previous recessionary phase of the national economy, it
was lower than the rate recorded in the years of major expansion.
This relative slow-down was, however, not brought about by the creation
of a substantial number of new non-agricultural jobs, especially in
industry, but coincided with a relatively smaller drift from the land.
The slowing down of migration from the South during the second half
of the 1960's, like the similar trend recorded during the first few
years of the above period, was not accompanied solely by a relative

MAP OF THE ITALIAN TERRITORIAL SUB-DIVISIONS

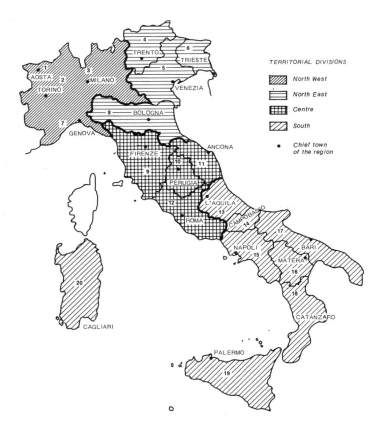

TERRITORIAL DIVISIONS

- North West
- North East
- Centre
- South
- • Chief town of the region

REGIONS

1. VAL D'AOSTA
2. PIEMONTE
3. LOMBARDIA
4. TRENTINO-ALTO ADIGE
5. VENETO
6. FRIULI-VENEZIA GIULIA
7. LIGURIA
8. EMILIA-ROMAGNA
9. TOSCANA
10. UMBRIA
11. MARCHE
12. LAZIO
13. ABRUZZO
14. MOLISE
15. CAMPANIA
16. BASILICATA
17. PUGLIA
18. CALABRIA
19. SICILIA
20. SARDEGNA

drop in rural migration, but also coincided with the growth of activities which provided a refuge, such as the retail trade and the civil service, and this was much more marked in the South than elsewhere. At the same time, there was a very substantial drop in the level of economic activity - at any rate much greater than in the rest of Italy.

Thus it can be seen that conditions have remained conducive to a continual shift in the population distribution, away from the South, though there was overall growth in the total.

Economic Changes

Despite the decline in the South's proportion of total population the region's share in the G. D. P. remained more or less constant, viz:

South

% of G. D. P.

1951	24.1
1958	24.0
1963	24.0
1966	24.2
1970	24.0
1971	24.3

The same is true of net per capita income, seen as a proportion of the national average, viz:

%

1951	62.7
1958	61.5
1963	61.9
1966	62.7
1970	62.5
1971	64.3

Since national income per head was rising over these years this shows that the South kept pace with Italy as a whole but the gap or disparity with the rest of Italy was not noticeably diminished. Although not sufficiently analytic, these figures do show that per capita income grew at the same rate in the South as in other parts of the country and this, during a twenty-year period when the Italian economy was growing fairly fast, is in itself a remarkable achievement.

While the disparity in income levels between the South and the rest of Italy is indicated by the measure of more than one third of the national average, it was even more marked by comparison with the North-West and North-East. In 1951 net per capita income in the South represented 40% of that in the North-West and 62% of that of the North-East. In 1970

it was 44% of that of the North-West but, because of a higher rate of
income growth in the North-East it was only 56% of that of that
group of regions. In 1971 it was 46.8% of the North-West and 60%
of the North-East.

Significantly, the rise in gross income was less in the South than
elsewhere. In the whole period 1951-1970 the average annual increase
in gross income for Italy as a whole was 5.6%. In the South however
it was 4.5%. The contraction in the rate of growth in 1970-71 to an
overall 1.3% affected the Northern regions rather than the South where
the rate fell to 3.4%.

The term "significantly" is emphasized since an important change
was nonetheless occurring in the twenty years from 1951, namely
a higher level of gross investment in the South than in Italy generally,
reflecting, undoubtedly, the positive efforts to overcome the basic
regional disparities by giving national priority to investment in the
South. During this period gross investment rose in the South at an
average annual rate of 9.0% compared with 7.3% in Italy as a whole
and 6.3% in the North-West and 7.4% in the North-East. While therefore it was not sufficient to alter the degree of disparity in net per
capita and gross incomes it still represented a rate of gross investment
of about one eighth more than the national average.

The reason for the apparent failure of high investment to lessen the
relative disparities may be discerned from an examination of the use to
which gross income is put, as between consumption, gross investment
and net exports.

A comparison of the years 1951, 1970 and 1971 shows the following:

USE OF INCOME BY REGIONAL GROUPS: CURRENT PRICES

(percentage gross income equals 100)

	1951		1970		1971	
	ITALY	SOUTH	ITALY	SOUTH	ITALY	SOUTH
Total consumption	81.1	98.9	85.2	93.9	78.1	93.8
Gross investment	20.2	19.7	22.7	29.4	20.3	27.4
Net exports*	- 1.4	-18.6	- 7.9	-23.3	1.6	-21.2
Gross income	100.0	100.0	100.0	100.0	100.0	100.0

*   The figure given after the minus sign indicates that there is a positive import balance.
     (This is in accordance with normal national accounting practice).

The South did not, in the post-war period, have the capacity for endogenous or self-generating growth but has depended on the import of capital and resources from outside - mainly from the rest of Italy but also of international capital. It shows also the relevance of the principles described in the "Re-appraisal", notably the interdependence of the South and the other regions. Without the overall growth of the national economy, inevitably originating in the more favoured Northern regions, the resources for the development of the South could not have been provided. Much of the total investment was by highly capital intensive firms, - a small proportion of firms representing a large proportion of the total investments. Investments by less capital intensive, smaller and locally based firms constituted a smaller proportion of the total. There was thus a structural imbalance, favouring the larger capital intensive investment (e.g. refineries) rather than the smaller locally based firms. In consequence, until local saving and capital accumulation can be combined with locally based skills and enterprise a large part of the return on investment will flow out from the South in the shape of profits, dividends and interest as well as a contribution to national revenues. In fact outflows of income from the South in the shape of profits and dividends on the substantial volume of imported capital has exceeded the remittances of emigrant workers. The post-war development of the South cannot be seen as a burden on the national economy but, insofar as a return on investment is sought and obtained, a contribution to its growth.

Another factor to be borne in mind is that a large proportion of the investment in the South, in infrastructure, land improvement and agriculture was directed to overcoming conditions of backwardness and obstacles to economic growth and was in a region of low labour productivity. The return on such investment, in measurable terms of G.D.P., was not likely to be as high as similar investment in those parts of Italy where conditions were more favourable to growth. This factor places also a limit on the extent to which resources could be devoted to the development of Southern Italy without undue detriment to the economic growth of the country as a whole.

The migrations from the South, while presenting social problems, can also be regarded as a contribution to national economic development, in that labour moved from regions of lower to regions of higher economic potential. Without such movement it is debatable whether the national economy could have expanded as much as it did, or that the North could have provided the surplus of resources needed for investment in the South.

Other Features of Regional Change

Between 1951 and 1970 there were noticeable changes in the regional structure of the economy and the regional distribution of the main sectors of economic activity. The industrial sector increased its contribution to G.D.P. from 36.7% in 1951 to

40.5% in 1970; the tertiary sector from 31.1% to 38.3%. On the other hand the contribution of agriculture fell from 22.9% to 10.3% - more than halving.

The effect was markedly different in the various regional groups. In the North West the share of agriculture of the regional G.D.P. fell from 14.3% to only 5.2%; in the North East from 28.7% to 12.6% and in the Centre from 19.4% to 8.0%. By contrast, in the South the fall, though significant, was smaller, from 34.0% to 17.8%.

The South participated however in the industrial growth of Italy, and both the industrial and tertiary sectors increased in importance in the region. In 1951 industry contributed 23.7% of the regional G.D.P. while by 1970 the proportion had risen to 29.2%. In the tertiary sector the proportions increased from 29.5% to 37.7%*. During the last four years of the period, value added by industry in the South increased at an average annual rate of 7.9% (compared with the national average of 8.1%, while in the period as a whole it increased by 7.4% against a national average of 7.5%). The contribution made to G.N.P. by the manufacturing industries increased from 13.2% in 1966 to 13.5% in 1970, the growth being marked in the more dynamic export industries, the more labour intensive industries such as mechanical engineering and vehicle building as well as modern capital intensive industries (metals, metal working, chemicals, etc.). There was in fact a more marked increase than in the rest of the country in the number of modern and technically more sophisticated industries, mainly capital intensive. They reflected substantial investment in larger scale enterprises in which a decisive contribution was made by enterprises in which the State had an interest.

Since the country's labour force did not expand, the increase, in output reflected a growth in productivity of labour, through increasing capital intensiveness, modernisation and improved techniques. Productivity in the South has however always tended to be lower than elsewhere. In 1951 it was estimated at 78.2% of the national average. In 1963 the ratio had slightly fallen, to 77.8%. In agriculture it fell slightly from 90.6% to 90% of the national average. In industry however productivity increase was most marked in the industrial North West, rising from 113.7% to 121.9%. In the South however it fell from 76.0% to 68.9% of the national average.

The picture had hardly changed by 1971. Productivity in all sectors in the South was 77.9% of the national average, 84.5% in agriculture and 71.7% in industry. Compared with the North West as a whole productivity in the South was only 62%, while in industrial activities the ratio was still lower (60%).

* The combined contributions in percentages of agriculture, industry and the tertiary sector to regional G.D.P. amounted to 87.2% in 1951 and to 84.7% in 1970; the differences are accounted for by the public sector.

It is clear that the comparatively low level of productivity in the South is not only a feature of its backwardness but a salient problem for regional policy. Since labour productivity is a function of capital investment, manpower utilisation as well as training, education and skills, it is not a problem for which there is a simple solution. It is clear however that there is a continuing need to give attention to all aspects of the productivity problem, if the South of Italy is ever to take an equal place in the general prosperity of the country.

Employment

The most marked change in the employment structure of Italy is the massive decline in agricultural employment and the corresponding shift to employment in industry and the tertiary sector. Between 1951 and 1970 agricultural employment fell close on 5 million, while employment in industry rose by 2.5 million and in tertiary activities by 1.85 million. (Overall there was a net fall of a quarter of a million). All regional groups shared in these massive changes:

EMPLOYMENT IN	1951-1970 (THOUSANDS)				
	NORTH WEST	NORTH EAST	CENTRE	SOUTH	TOTAL
Agriculture ...	-128	-1,206	-1,079	-1,851	-4,957
Industry	801	587	418	589	2,486
Tertiary activities ...	455	384	137	474	1,853
General Government .	131	107	131	233	652
Total	566	- 163	- 103	- 545	- 246

The overall net loss of employment in the South was matched by an almost equal gain in the North West, the other two regional groups accounting for the net overall loss of employment in the country as a whole. The South's share of national employment fell from 33.0% in 1951 to 30.6% in 1970.

While all regional groups gained in industrial employment the gain was higher in the North West. In the industrial sector however there was a marked contrast between manufacturing and construction.

Whereas three quarters of the industrial growth in the North West was in manufacturing, in the South more than this proportion was in construction. Non-agricultural jobs in the South increased by 1.3 million but more than half - about 725 thousand - was in construction and commerce which both show some instability as regards employment and organisation as well as having levels of productivity similar in many respects to those in agriculture.

INDUSTRIES	1951-1970 (THOUSANDS)				
	NORTH WEST	NORTH EAST	CENTRE	SOUTH	TOTAL
Manufacturing ..	614	446	279	161	1,601
Construction ...	165	135	137	429	867

The effect of these changes was that, by 1970 half (49.6%) of Italy's agricultural employment was located in the South, compared with 42.6% in 1951. Though the South's proportion of national employment in industry had marginally increased (from 22.5% to 23.2%) its proportion of manufacturing employment fell, from 19.5% to 17.3%. In construction employment, however, the proportion increased from 33.3% to 39.8%, while the proportion in tertiary activities was more or less static (27.8% of the national total compared with 27.4% in 1951).

Nonetheless, in the South itself, the national trend towards a declining proportion of employment in agriculture and increasing proportions in industry and the tertiary sectors was also reflected, though to a less degree.

EMPLOYMENT BY SECTORS AS A PROPORTION OF TOTAL EMPLOYMENT

	1951		1970	
	SOUTH	ITALY	SOUTH	ITALY
Agriculture	56.7	43.9	30.8	19.0
Industry	20.1	29.4	32.0	42.2
Manufacturing ..	13.4	22.6	17.3	30.8
Construction	5.5	5.6	13.2	10.2
Tertiary activities ..	17.4	20.9	26.9	29.6
General Government .	5.8	5.8	10.3	9.2
Total	100.0	100.0	100.0	100.0

It can be seen, therefore, that the South, broadly speaking, moved, in respect of the employment structure, in the same directions as the rest of the country, though with a smaller rise in the proportion of

41

manufacturing employment and a larger rise in construction and the tertiary and general government sectors (both relatively low income producing sectors and liable to instability).

Industrial Investment

It is to be noted that in the two decades from 1951 the South took an increasing proportion of national gross investment in the industrial sector. In 1951 the South's proportion of the total was 14.9%; in 1964 it had reached a peak of 30.25%. Over the period as a whole it averaged 21.8% - being under 20% in the years to 1962 and substantially exceeding that proportion in subsequent years.

In absolute terms gross industrial investment in the South increased from 105 thousand million lire in 1951 to 701 thousand million lire in 1969 - almost a sevenfold increase, whereas for Italy as a whole the increase was from 703 thousand million lire to 2,767 thousand million lire, not quite four-fold.

The growth in industrial investment was not, of course, steady. Fluctuations in the state of the national economy, in the provisions for investment in the South and in the rate of development combined to produce variations in the rate of increase. In some years (1955, 1960-63) the annual increase was particularly high (over 40 thousand million lire in 1955, 1962 and 1963) while in seven of the years there was actually a decline (particularly large in 1965). As has been noted in the "Reappraisal", the susceptibility of the economy to upswings and downswings can have a marked effect on the impact of regional policies, which is not immune to factors affecting the economy as a whole. In years when the country's rate of economic growth falls off, or at least fails to rise, the consequences are more marked in the South, and the smaller enterprises are particularly hard hit. They are, of course, structurally weaker from both the financial and the technical and administrative point of view. In addition, there is a cyclical time lag between the successive phases of the trend of economic activity and the level of investment in the South.

The general conclusions to be drawn from this survey is that the two decades saw substantial advances in the economy of the South, in diversifying the economy and reducing the dependence on agriculture, increasing incomes, productivity and investment, especially in construction but also in large scale and capital intensive manufacturing industry. But the changes were not sufficient to modify the imbalance between the South and the North and in this respect the problem for regional policy remained, continuing to create pressure on the active population to seek better opportunities elsewhere, not only in Italy but in other countries.

C. THE DEVELOPMENT OF THE APPROACH TO REGIONAL POLICIES

The nature and scale of the problems of the South, and the degree of national imbalance, once recognised, not only called for a wide range of policies but their continual modification and adaptation in the light of the evolution of the national conditions and the results achieved. Objectives, policies and measures therefore changed and developed as the lessons of experience were gathered and evaluated. Perhaps, nowhere more than in Italy, is the principle illustrated that the aim of modifying large scale imbalances in regional economic structure (and accompanying social imbalances) requires a substantial, continuing, determined long term effort, and one which comprehends study and research, elaboration of strategies and specific measures, the allocation of substantial resources and attention to a wide range of interconnected subjects, from national infrastructure development, regional physical planning, promotion of education, training and health facilities to the development of organisations and institutions capable of devising, coordinating and implementing the variety of tasks which have to be undertaken. All these elements feature in the Italian approach to regional policies*.

Post-war regional policy can be said to have been initiated in the period 1947-53. Study and recognition of the nature of the problem of imbalance led to legislation in 1950 which provided for the codification of the whole of the South into a regional entity - the Mezzogiorno, the establishment of a special fund, financed from the national budget - the "Cassa per il Mezzogiorno", the preparation of an organic pluriennial "plan" (initially for ten years) for which responsibility was allotted to the Cassa as an autonomous public agency under the political direction of a "Committee of Ministers for the South".

Other elements in this initial phase included measures of land reform not only in the South but all areas where large landed estates were prevalent and used for extensive agriculture. About 500,000 hectares were expropriated in the South and 200,000 hectares in Central and Northern Italy, to be improved and developed into small holdings and then allocated to about 100,000 peasant families. They also included a number of financial measures, ranging from ten-year fiscal exemptions for new industrial enterprises established in the South, procurement of foreign loans, to be administered by the Cassa, establishment of credit institutes for the mainland South, Sicily and Sardinia, and the provision of funds for the ten year plan for the South as well as for public works in mountain communes and other depressed areas.

* Only a brief outline is possible here. For more details the reader is referred to the reports "Latest Results and New Features of Official Action in the Mezzogiorno (Italy), OECD, October 1973 and "Salient Features of Regional Development Policy in Italy", OECD, July 1970.

One thousand billion lire (about 1% of national income) were
provided for the first ten year Plan 1950-60, essentially for the
development of infrastructures and modifications of the environment.
Three quarters was to be devoted to agriculture, mountain land
consolidation, irrigation, agricultural reform and incentives for farm
transformation; the remainder was utilised for road and water development and minor works in the field of tourism.

Although some initial steps were taken for the development of a
specific industrial policy, this first Plan was concerned with, and
implemented essentially as a "preindustrialisation" plan.

In 1957 the life time of the Plan was extended to fifteen years (to
1965). Appropriations to the Cassa were increased (to 2,300 billion
lire - about $ 3,650 million) and the legislation provided for the
promotion of industrialisation in Southern Italy by considerable incentives borne by the Cassa, by territorial planning - concentration
of industrial plants in selected areas and "nuclei" assisted by investment in infrastructures (ports, roads, rail links, industrial estates)
and by measures for improving human capabilities (training in labour
and business skills, etc.).

The results of the first twelve years of action were impressive
by any standards. The progressive deterioration of the South had been
halted, incomes were rising at the rate of 4% per annum (still, however,
lower than the national rate); with the elimination of malaria and the
partition of the latifundia about 2 million hectares of plainlands had
been rendered capable of intensive cultivation; 8,000 km of new roads
opened up; and new water supply systems created for 850 communes.

But large scale emigration persisted (about 1.7 million leaving
the South to the North and abroad) and there had been no reduction in
the economic and social gap between the two areas.

A number of weaknesses of the system were however becoming
apparent.

i) Difficulties in achieving adequate coordination between the
special fund and other investments from the normal budgets
of Ministries.

ii) Consequently difficulty in securing that an adequate proportion
of Government Departmental expenditure was allocated to the
South. (As noted in "Issues of Regional Policies"* and in
the Re-appraisal, the danger of special funds is that they may
result in a reduction of expenditure from normal funds or
budgets).

iii) The delay in the start of industrialisation measures to comple-
ment action in the field of infrastructure and agriculture.

iv) The absence of a regional "multiplier" effect of infrastructure
investment and agricultural development, the high proportion

---

* Issues of Regional Policies, OECD, 1973.

of income induced outside the area, the social obstacles to small enterprise, the high capital/income ratio of investments and low rates of local capital formation and industrialisation.

The two main requirements, demonstrated by experience - better coordination and a faster rate of industrial development - led to the conclusion that a national rather than a purely regional planning policy was required.

The first National Economic Plan, for 1966-70, was launched by a law of 1967. The expiry of the Plan for Southern Italy in 1965 necessitated the introduction of a revised plan in 1965, consistent with the anticipated objectives of the National Plan.

The two laws provided for intensification and extension of the policies for the South, including greater public and private investment with special regard to industrialisation; strengthening of the incentive system; extending the period for planning to 1980, renewing the mandate of the Cassa; closer coordination of public and private investment in the South, a forward looking (ex ante) formulation of pluriennial programmes (rather than the corrective, ex post approach of the past); and the coordination of regional planning and national planning by the integration of the former Committee of Ministers for the South into a new Committee for National Economic Planning (CIPE-- Comitato Inter-Ministeriale Planificazione Economiche). Provision was also made for greater utilisation of the "State Holdings" instrument for pruposes of industrialisation of the South (leading to large scale projects of State Holdings enterprise such as doubling of capacity of the Taranto steel complex, large motor vehicle plant in Naples, aluminium plant in Sardinia, petrochemical complexes at Gela, Manfredonia, etc.).

Not only were increased appropriations made for the Cassa and for various pluriennial programmes of Ministries, for school buildings, ports, roads, railways, etc. but a new provision of law was the requirement for the obligatory allocation of at least 40% of investment expenditure by all Public Departments and by the large State enterprises (ENEL, ENI, CNEN, IRI, etc.) to Southern Italy.

The five year programme (1965-69) provided in total for expenditure of 1,900 billion lire in direct Cassa liabilities and 4,000 billion in overall investment promotion.

The basic lines of action or strategy involved the adoption of increasingly complex and far reaching formulae, summarised as:

i) Greater concentration of growth in preferential areas (development poles) of specialised and integrated projects.

ii) Rational planning of various aspects of correlation between public infrastructures and incentives and productive investment. This system, in which Italy has been an originator, is known as "contrattazione programmata" - planned agreement for

45

specific projects between Government, management and labour. It facilitates the development and coordination of public and private aspects of major projects in accordance with local planning policies.

iii) Increasing attention to the collateral aspects of physical investment, i.e. research, universities, training and education, market organisation (technical and organisational assistance to enterpreneurs and local authorities).

The first phase of planning for the South (1950-65) can be said to have identified the areas displaying the specific characteristics of depressed territories in which intervention could best be concentrated. The plan was a regional plan, limited to one part of the country and did not form part of an overall national plan. In the second phase, from 1965, regional action was integrated with the comprehensive National Development Plan. The objectives, in both cases, however, were, by means of increased investment, both in fixed social capital* and directly productive projects, and through higher productivity, to raise the level of incomes to the point at which savings start to develop, thus creating an autonomous growth mechanism.

However, at the stage reached so far, it relies predominantly on the contribution of capital from outside (as an average the overall deficit of Southern Italy has been about 25% of the total amount of resources of the region which was covered by the inflow from outside). This heavy dependence on outside resources was of great importance in determining the type of measures (public capital investments, incentives to industrialists, etc.) which were needed to implement the general policy.

Diversion of resources to the Region, to be effective, required to be complemented by elaboration of local plans for the utilisation of the resources available. These were formulated in respect of the major economic sectors, agriculture, industry and tourism. Within this framework studies and planning were developed for land reclamation and irrigation districts, for industrial development areas and for tourist development districts. The approach was selective, concentrating on the areas judged to be the most suitable. In this way a "regional plan" or strategy was evolved, in which resource allocation and phasing could reflect the priorities between the individual projects.

The various combined "sectorial-territorial" components (land reclamation districts, industrial areas and nuclei, tourist industry development districts), and interrelation of infrastructure and economic development and the overlapping of areas capable of more than one type of sectoral development, in practice resulted in large "development poles". Apart from the geographical factors this process reflects

---

*   Fixed capital used for the provision of services to the collectivity, e.g. houses, hospitals, schools, roads, etc.

46

the agglomerative trend of fixed social capital and the economies of
scale through concentration of services. A series of close interrela-
tionships also arises between the programme for the provision of
infrastructures for servicing the economic requirements of the "pole"
and the town planning and highways programmes for urban and extra-
urban areas.

The role of the State outside the provision of budgetary funds
deserves special mention. The traditional reluctance of private
industry in the North to move to the South increased the importance
of intervention through the State holding enterprises. Intervention
was both direct, by public and semi-public agencies, and indirect, by
the creation of private statutory companies formed with major State
holding of equity. Legislation provided that the activities of these
agencies and the relative investment should be concentrated in the
South (at least 60% of new investment).

Another intermediate form of venture is represented by the Joint
Financing Companies (an industrial and an agricultural company) in
which the Cassa has a major holding. These companies subscribe,
normally with a minority holding to the authorised (risk) capital of
enterprises engaged in new development and capable of providing
practical impetus, with "know-how", to sectors and investments which
are especially complex and difficult for private enterprise to develop
unaided.

Other elements in the strengthened approach to regional policy
included the establishment under the Cassa of an autnomous Training
and Study Centre (in Naples) and an Institute for Assistance to the
Development of Southern Italy (IASMA) having the objectives of promotion of industry and tourism facilities.

In the more recent phase in the evolution of regional policies
further steps were taken to strengthen the regional element in national
planning.

One of the most significant innovations is the introduction of the
regional system for the whole country. This is still in an early and
experimental stage of setting up regional authorities, determining
the financial resources for the individual regions and transferring
certain State functions to the latter. It is, however, too early to make
any precise economic evaluation of the scheme. The list of regions
is shown on the Map. The functions are listed in Art. 117 of the
Constitution which gave regional bodies independent powers in certain
sectors of production (in particular, in the agricultural sector), and
with regard to questions of social policy and everything to do with area
redevelopment and town and country planning. In addition, the State
can delegate further responsibilities to the regions by legislative and
administrative means. The question of financial resources was dealt
with by means of special legislation. The arrangement is based on
a mixed system of State allocations, determined according to parameters established in advance, and State contributions levied directly

by the regions for their use. More specifically, the system of parameters is as follows : 1) resident population; 2) surface area; 3) level of migration; 4) level of unemployment; 5) individual tax burden resulting from income tax.

The main features of the legislation of 1971 in regard to the South were to establish a more direct relationship between action for the South and national economic programming; to give the Cassa a more pronounced "agency" function; to improve and amplify the operational arrangements of an industrial and regional nature. These affect financial incentives, infrastructure projects, technical assistance and training and participation by State enterprise as well as administrative procedures.

The law specifically recognised (for the first time) that the development of Southern Italy is a fundamental objective of national economic planning.

The tasks of CIPE were more specifically defined to cover a wide range of directives. The role of the Central Ministry of Planning was widened to include establishing directives to replace the pluriennial coordination plans and approving special projects formulated by the Minister for Intervention in the South or by Southern regional authorities.

Of especial interest is the introduction of the power of CIPE to control the location of large new industrial plants or their extension, CIPE permission being required for investments exceeding 7 billion lire , with penalties equal to 25% of the investment in cases of infringement.

Participation by the regions themselves is provided by the establishment of a Committee consisting of Chairmen of the Councils of the Southern regions, with power to make proposals and advise on matters submitted to the CIPE. The regions were also to share in the responsibility for compilation of development programmes.

The scale of financing of the region was raised to 7,200 billion lire for the five years 1971-75. For the ten years up to the end of 1973 the total investments made, or encouraged, amounted to 12,600 billion lire. The distribution of this total, under main headings, was as follows:

(000 billion lire)

General Infrastructure	1.6
Agriculture	2.1
Industry	7.6
Tourism	0.5
Handicrafts and Fisheries ...	0.4
Technical Progress and Civil Development	0.2
Areas of special depression .	0.1

A wide variety of other measures was adopted, including those in the incentives field and particularly to encourage small enterprise, to promote industrialisation in inland areas, to foster handicrafts, commerce and tourism and facilitate efficient operation of industry (especially in large firms). To sum up, regional policies have evolved since their inception in the early post-war years. The direction has been towards increasing the scale of intervention for the benefit of the South and improving and widening the range of instruments for increasing investment especially from outside the region, and for developing a comprehensive national/regional planning system and appropriate institutions. While there have undoubtedly been positive results the continued development of policies and instruments reflects awareness of the fact that, so far, the main objective of narrowing the economic and social gap between the South and the rest of the country remains a task which still has to be accomplished.

D. THE INSTRUMENTS OF REGIONAL POLICY

The instruments of regional policy comprise a wide range of measures intended to promote and facilitate investment, extending from fiscal concessions to the orientation of Government investment to the development of infrastructures and fixed social capital. The variety of measures involves the intervention of many and varied bodies (Ministries, regional administrations, State holdings). But, apart from the vital fundamental fiscal concessions the major weight of responsibility and financial commitments has rested with the Cassa, within the appropriation made from the national budget.

The direct interventions concerned can be grouped into two categories:

a)   incentives aimed at reducing the burden of investment in new projects and operating costs in the early years;

b)   the assumption, total or partial, of the costs of specific infrastructures and of fixed social capital for the servicing of industrial development.

Indirect intervention is effected by a number of legislative provisions designed to guide both public and private investment towards the South. Thus the 1965 legislation introduced the obligatory allocation of at least 40% of investment expenditure by all Public Departments and State agencies and enterprises in Southern Italy. In addition, 30% of contracts of supply to Government Departments and public agencies were to be placed in the South. The most recent legislation added the provision that sums not used within the 40% rule by the end of the year should be spent on special projects, while the obligatory percentage of industrial investments by the administrative agencies and Government controlled enterprises in the South was raised to 80% for new plants. The investments of these agencies and firms in the South will also have to account for a share of not less than 60% of their total investments in new undertakings.

Apart from these measures of a financial type a further instrument of guidance is the introduction of the new rules requiring Government authority for the establishment or extension of large undertakings, applying to all companies with a share capital of over 5 billion lire and projects exceeding 7 billion lire. The criteria allow account to be taken of national planning directives.

Lastly, planning policies and machinery have been increasingly geared to securing a balanced territorial distribution of the productive apparatus of the country. While, in the earlier years, these related primarily to planning at the regional level, through coordinated development of local preferential areas the planning system also now requires a coordination of national development strategy through the system of "special projects of organic intervention". Under this system the choice of "intermediate" objectives must comply with the general targets of economic development and territorial adjustment (as well as practicalities) and relate not only to intersectoral development in the South but elsewhere.

As has been noted the scale of financial provision for the South has been progressively increased. For the 1971-75 Plan the total provision was raised to some 7,200 billion lire, including the direct expenditure and commitments of the Cassa and concessions of interest on loans. This sum exceeded the amount hitherto committed throughout the previous 20 years (up to 1970 some 6,610 thousand billion had been provided in credits to the Cassa).

Incentives to firms

The system of incentives has varied over time. It has included grants towards interest on loans and towards capital expenditure; services and guarantees on international loans; participation in risk capital, reduction of tax reliefs of various kinds (reductions and period exemptions of income and company tax) and concessions in certain types of charges (duties on transfers of land and buildings, general transaction tax on plant machinery, social security contributions, etc.); a system of capital grants and loans at reduced rates, for industrial and commercial firms, varying from 35% (45% in areas of marked depopulation) of fixed investments in the case of smaller firms (with a capital up to 1.5 billion lire) through 15%-20% in the case of medium size firms (with a capital up to 5 billion lire) and, between 7% and 12% in the case of larger firms (the last subject to negotiation within the planned agreement system). The grants are increased by 10% where certain equipment is constructed in Southern Italy.

Loans at reduced rates can also be granted for commercial firms engaged in distribution.

The system is therefore a clearly graduated one, according to the size of firms, and is now weighted more heavily towards the smaller firms.

Precise evaluation of the value of these incentives to firms is difficult to make, but there seems little doubt that they are among the most important of the instruments at present in use.

Other financial aid to development

The second, and also important financial method is the aid of the Cassa itself to infrastructure and social equipment in the South. Under the 1965 Plan the Cassa was enabled to assume the residual cost and subsequently, the total cost of specific infrastructures in industrial "areas or nuclei". In addition it could provide grants for housing for workers, for industrial buildings, water storage, etc., up to 30-50%, as well as to establish centres for vocational training, training courses, social centres, technical assistance, etc. However, this sort of operation was in fact very rare.

Investment by the Cassa in infrastructure had reached a total of 1,928 billion lire by 1967 while grant-aided private investment reached a total of 4,000 billion showing the changed scope for industrial growth after the initial pre-industrialisation era, in which the main emphasis, as noted earlier, was in agriculture and infrastructure. Data for recent years, which confirms this trend are shown on Table 2· In total, investment by the Cassa up to the end of 1973 amounted to 12,600 billion.

E. DEVELOPMENT OF METHODOLOGY

The policies outlined in the previous sections indicate clearly a process of evolution in methods to give them effect. In the course of time, changes were made in administratives principles and procedures, and in the range, scale and scope of the various instruments, in order to make them more effective and to apply the lessions of experience. The need to adapt and change methods in the light of experience is of course itself a basic principle of the methodology of regional policy, and Italy provides perhaps one of the most fruitful fields for study by those interested in such questions, including Governments which are at an earlier stage in the development of regional policies.

The salient features of the methodology of Italian regional policy can be summarised under a number of main heads:

   i)   Administrative machinery and procedures
  ii)   Resource management
 iii)   Investment guidance
 iv)   Study (research, diagnosis, appraisal and evaluation).

Table 2. INVESTMENTS COMPLETED OR ENCOURAGED AT END DECEMBER 1973

(billion Lire)

SECTORS	IN 1971	IN 1972	IN 1973[e]	AT 31st DECEMBER 1973
General Infrastructure ...	165	191	194	1,615
Water supply and drainage	104	121	121	942
Roads and railways ..	52	65	66	619
Hospitals	9	5	7	54
Agriculture	122	138	161	2,109
Infrastructure	73	87	93	1,405
Land improvement[a] ..	49	51	68	704
Industry	1,058	1,251	1,039	7,649
Infrastructure	48	57	69	259
Plant[b]	1,010	1,194[e]	970	7,390
Tourism	61	69	58	454
Infrastructure	9	10	12	104
Hotel and tourist development[c]......	52	59	46	350
Crafts and fisheries[d]	22	57	41	436
Technical progress and Civil Development	19	19	24	230
Special depressed areas ..	18	33	50	108
TOTAL	1,465	1,758	1,567	12,601

a) Includes investment for land improvement, grain stores, earthquake damage, technical assistance and co-operatives for processing and storing agricultural products.
b) Net of stocks and working capital.
c) Includes hotels and other tourist development works.
d) This series replaces previously published data.
e) Provisional.

i) Administrative machinery and procedures

A number of features can be noted which themselves reflect the magnitude of the regional problem and the fact that it involved action at national and regional level.

First, is the creation of special machinery at central Government level, initially the establishment of the Committee of Ministers for the South and subsequently its integration into the national economic planning machinery of the CIPE. This illustrates two principles: that the nature and scale of the problem called for more effective machinery than could be provided by the normal allocation of responsibilities between separate "functional" Ministries, even acting in consultation; and that (by the creation and role of CIPE) regional policy needed to be fully integrated and coordinated with national policy. The machinery permitted the enunciation of policy objectives and directives, as well as supervision of the Ministries, agencies and institutions, all involved in a concerted national effort for the regeneration and development of the South and other areas requiring special attention within the national framework.

Second, is the establishment of special agencies, notably the Cassa and its related bodies, to give impetus by funds and promotional activities, to the specific objectives of the policy laid down by the supreme State authorities.

Third, is the utilisation, for purpose of regional policies, of other State agencies, notably the State holding enterprises, under policy directives and in conjunction with the special regional agencies.

Fourth, is the development of machinery at regional level, to ensure the study of local conditions, to define objectives and to formulate plans. As has been noted, evolution is towards increasing the responsibility of local authorities and bodies while ensuring coordination with central aims and policies.

Overall it can be said that machinery has been developed to ensure that regional objectives are defined and find their place in national objectives, that there is coordination at national and regional levels, and between them, and that the administrative agencies are available for the implementation of policies.

No doubt further changes may be found necessary - no administrative system is ever final - but the developments outlined indicate the importance that is attached to devising adequate machinery for the tasks which regional policies pose in the conditions of Italy.

ii) Resource management

The primary feature of resource management in Italian regional policy is the specific allocation of financial resources from the national budget to the development agencies, initially the Cassa for the South, but also for the pluriennial programmes of central Government Departments, the additional regional programmes for Sicily, Sardinia, Calabria and for mountain communes and depressed areas of Central and Northern Italy. This method for providing resources is of allied nature to the administrative structure adopted, but, at the same time, it indicates acceptance of the principle of special budgeting as an essential means of providing the resources required, or that can be made available, for the policies and programmes of regional development which fall outside the "normal" budgeting of individual Ministries.

The case for such a system may be said to be based on two fundamental considerations. First, the inescapable need for a special effort for promoting the development of the South. This was seen, not only as in the interest of the South but as a means for widening the base of the national economy too heavily concentrated in the North. Secondly, experience had shown that, without special measures, resources, including public investment, would continue to flow most strongly towards the more economically developed regions.

Of interest from a methodological standpoint is however the fact that the creation of special funds had an initially adverse effect, in the sense that, after its creation, the tendency of central Government Departments was to respond more fully to requests from the Northern regions, which, unlike those in the South, could not count on additional resources. Because of this tendency it became necessary to supplement the special fund with the rule requiring 40% of investment by Ministries to be located in the South.

While there is no way of knowing what course ordinary public investment would have followed if there had not been a special plan backed by allocated resources, the evidence suggests that the creation of the fund and the 40% rule were essential to the policy. However it should be noted that the 40% rule could not be consistently applied. Similarly, in the private sector the normal tendency of industry to invest in existing advanced regions leads to the supposition that a strong incentive policy, backed by the allocated funds was also essential.

iii) Investment guidance

As has been noted, the methods for guiding investment to the South are several. In the public sector, they include the direct allocation of funds, the statutory proportions required by Ministries, agencies and State enterprises and the more recent measures for controlling the location of large enterprises. The methods are therefore both positive and negative, incentives and restraints. It is too early to evaluate the effect of the restraint measures. Significant for methodology is however the fact that restraints have been introduced at a relatively late stage, and that (unlike, e.g. in the United Kingdom) they are limited to very large undertakings. Also, in common with some other countries such restraints as these are discretionary and may serve other purposes (such as local planning, avoidance of congestion in urban areas) than the guidance of industry to one special part of the country.

iv) Study

This is noted under "methodology" to draw attention to the importance attached to the "intelligence" aspect of regional policy, the gathering and elaboration of data, the appraisal and evaluation of experience and trends and the formulation of plans and projects based on careful study of the economic and social aspects of the problems involved. A considerable number of organisations and institutions, of high quality, have been created at both central Government and regional level. The development of a forward looking, or ex ante, approach is perhaps less advanced than the study and appraisal of past trends, but it already plays a part in the pluriennial regional plans. The value of the studies undertaken is shown by the relevance of the actions that have taken place under their influence. The greater momentum that has already been achieved in the development of the South, and the realisation that much remains to be accomplished, suggest that there will be an increasing need to develop existing forecasting techniques so that the problems of the future can be prepared for.

F. CONCLUSIONS DRAWN FROM EXPERIENCE

The evolution of policies and methodologies enable a number of main conclusions to be formulated from Italian experience.

First, that the scale of the problem of the South, to which must be added problems of depressed or backward areas within the centre and the North, cannot be successfully tackled by a piecemeal and ad hoc approach to the problems in a purely local regional setting. The background of national growth, and the in-built tendencies to more rapid development of the more favoured regions, under the influence also of international competition (which itself favours economically more advanced regions) called for an increasingly comprehensive approach in which regional and national policies were integrated within a common framework.

Secondly, the wide range of matters to be dealt with at regional level [infrastructure, land reform, urban development, localisation of industry in selected areas, social development (education, housing, etc)] required a system of coordination - between public authorities and industry, between regional and central bodies and at the centre itself. This system of coordination was not only in the field of institutions and administrative procedures but in methods of economic and physical planning, to ensure rational local development, linking it with the national superstructure of roads, ports and harbours, power supplies and ensuring a balanced "mix" of large scale and medium size undertakings and the facilitation or promotion of local enterprise as well as imported.

Thirdly, the different instruments were likely to be effective only in combination with each other - neither incentives to induce a flow of capital investment, nor attention to infrastructures and planning programmes would be sufficient by themselves to secure the progress aimed at.

Fourthly, to be noted is the close interdependence between national and regional growth. The dependence of the South on the resources that could be steered from elsewhere required growth in the North as well as the South, and the rate of growth and of investment that could be achieved in the South required a balancing of the needs of all parts of the country. In theory regional policy could be pursued to a point at which national growth could suffer from the excessive diversion of resources, from high return to low return regions. But to do so could imperil national advancement and the ability to increase resources for the development of the South. Conversely the development of the South is to be seen not as a burden on, but as a contribution to the strengthening of the national economy by bringing into it the under-developed resources of such a substantial proportion of the country. This can be regarded as further evidence of the need for the close coordination of national and regional economic policies in conditions prevailing in Italy.

A further conclusion that can be drawn from the experience of the two decades of active regional policy is that, while it has been possible to make absolute progress in the South comparable, or perhaps slightly exceeding, that of the rest of Italy, the relative gap has remained virtually unchanged. This does not mean that the effort and results in the South have not been significant or impressive. The contrary is true. It means however that growth has also continued at a high rate elsewhere, because of the relatively more favourable conditions. It would seem that means should be found for enabling the internal capability of Southern Italy to be expanded more rapidly than the rest of the country, by encouraging small and locally based enterprises, by a higher rate of local capital accumulation and a faster rate of improvement in skills and local enterprise than elsewhere, or, alternatively, of diverting a still greater proportion of national resources to the South than has been achieved in the past two decades. Unless this is done there is little prospect of a significant narrowing of the relative disparities between the South and the rest of Italy. The integration of the national economy in the international market, in its turn, should not be an obstacle but should support this fundamental necessity (of a structural rather than "regional" character). It is not suprising therefore that increasing emphasis is placed in Italy on large scale international collaboration, by a new orientation of EEC policies and by the regional fund of the EEC, to overcome the basic imbalance between North and South and to encourage the enlargement and diversification of Europe's economic and social base.

G. EXPECTATIONS

Although progress has been achieved in the South in the past twenty years - progress which had not previously occurred since the inception of the Italian State - it would seem clear that the problem of the South, as regards both the low level of economic and social development, and the relative disparity between the South and elsewhere, is likely to remain a feature of Italy for many years to come. The point at which growth in the South is sufficient to overcome the general conditions of backwardness and to achieve a self-sustaining and considerably higher rate of progress than elsewhere is not yet foreseeable. In this connection, continuance and intensification of the policies already in operation would seem essential. Essential also is the need to analyse the effects of national policies which do not directly concern the South. Of key importance, however, is the progress already achieved, viz. the existence of large basic industries; the communications improvements that have brought Southern Italy "nearer" to the main centres of development; the increasing attention being paid to the fostering of local capital accumulation and enterprise; the availability of manpower and improved skills and productivity; the advanced state of large hydrological schemes; and the attention now being given to agriculture (both intensive and extensive). All this offers some hope that a more acceptable level of economic and social life can be reached long before there is "parity" between North and South. This prospect may however depend on whether it becomes possible, through the EEC, to internationalise the approach to Italy's problem of the South and to achieve harmonious and balanced expansion of the EEC itself.

III

IRELAND

A. THE NATIONAL PERSPECTIVE OF REGIONAL POLICIES

The population of Ireland is approximately 3 million (3.086 million in 1974). Its growth rate over the decade to 1974 averaging 0.77% annually is above those of Austria, Finland and Belgium but below those of France, Germany, Italy, the Netherlands, Norway and the United Kingdom. It has had however the highest natural growth rate among EEC countries excepting the Netherlands but also the highest net emigration rate, exceeding that of Italy. Between 1961 and 1971 there was a net emigration of 134,500 representing an annual average of 0.5% though this period saw a marked decline compared with the previous decade in which the average rate was 1.4%.

Ireland is also a country of low population density, with 44 inhabitants per sq.km. (less than half that of France, less than a quarter of that of Italy).

The 1973 working population, of 1.1 million or one third of the total, compares with 1.3 million in 1950, 1.1 million in 1960 and 1.1 million in 1969.

In structural terms it remains heavily dependent on the primary sector (agriculture, forestry and fishing). In 1974 the proportion of employment in this sector was 24.0%, though in keeping with trends elsewhere the sector has declined in relative importance, from 37.3% in 1960 and 28.4% in 1969. By contrast the proportion in the secondary (industry) sector has risen to 30.8% in 1974 compared with 23.7% in 1960; while tertiary employment has risen from 39% in 1960 to 45.2% in 1974. Unemployment has however tended to be high, averaging 5.0% in 1966-71. Since mid-April 1974 the unemployment rate has climbed to around 10%.

Average income per head is the lowest in the EEC countries. In terms of GDP the low earning power of agriculture is shown by the fact that this sector contributed only 19.4% of the GDP (1973). However, agriculture accounted for over 37% of total merchandise exports in 1974.

The past decade however has seen substantial general economic progress. Notable features have been:

- the first sustained increase in population for over a hundred years;
- an average annual GNP growth of 4.3% (at constant prices) in 1960-73;
- an average annual growth rate of 6% (at constant prices) in the product of the industrial sector in the period 1960-72;
- the rise in the proportion of population in the industrial sector;
- a reduction in net emigration;
- an average annual growth rate of about 8.5% in gross domestic fixed capital formation between 1960 and 1974, the investment rates (fixed capital formation as a percentage of GDP) rising from 13.3% in 1958 to around 24.6% in 1974.

Nevertheless the Irish economy must still rank as under-developed and in need of continuing structural transformation, while the pace of growth is constrained by the limited availability of capital. Despite sizeable capital inflows there was also a net foreign disinvestment* in 1972 estimated at 10% of the gross total available for investment.

B. THE EMERGENCE OF REGIONAL PROBLEMS AND THEIR NATURE

The regional distribution of the population is a reflection of its economy. Since industrial and service employment are mainly urban in character the density of population is considerably higher in the areas of regions containing the two largest towns, Dublin (568,000) and Cork (129,000), and lower in the mainly agricultural areas with smaller towns and villages, there being no major city inland. Over a third (35.7%) of the population is located in the East region, while the East and South East regions together account for nearly half (46.78) (See Table 1**). The East region containing Dublin, is the only region in which population density exceeds the national average, being, at 152 per sq. km., nearly four times as high. The tendency towards greater concentration in the East region is marked. It is the only region whose share of the total population grew between 1966 and 1971 and the only one with a positive migration flow, (see Table 4) internal migration towards Dublin more than offsetting emigration from Dublin.

As can be seen from Table 1 considerable variations also exist in population density in the regions outside the East, varying from as low of 22 per sq. km in Donegal to 43 per sq. km in the North East.

---

*   Foreign disinvestment is measured as the reduction of external reserves arising from a deficit in the Balance of International Payments on Current Account. This does not indicate that there was a net withdrawal by foreign investors of investment in Ireland.
    **   The Tables and Maps are appended.

In the "designated" areas as a whole (i.e. Regions Donegal, North-West together with parts of regions North-East, Midlands Mid-West and South-West) containing 32% of the population in 1966 and 31% in 1971, the average density in 1971 was 24 per sq. km compared with 66 per sq. km in the rest of the country.

Differences in regional economic conditions are shown equally clearly by Tables 3 and 5.

Here again, the East region, containing Dublin not only has the highest proportion of working population in industry and services but is the only region in which personal income per capita exceeds the national average, the difference being greater still in the case of Dublin City and County.

However, all parts of Ireland have benefitted from and contributed to economic growth at national level. During the sixties the percentage increases in real personal incomes per head achieved in the various areas did not vary markedly. In general the underdeveloped areas achieved a rate of growth in per capita incomes similar to that recorded in the more advanced regions. But, since the initial incomes in the former case were lower, the absolute gap in incomes between the two areas has widened somewhat, though not to a large extent. In the industrially underdeveloped areas the development of agriculture, tourism, forestry and sea fishing play a significant role.

Two other elements in the regional situation should be noted. The existence of a border with Northern Ireland has been a significant influence on the development of certain regions through its economic and political effects. Secondly, a larger proportion of new industry is promoted by foreign interest whose willingness to promote projects in Ireland can be influenced by the degree to which they are left free to determine their location.

What, to some extent at least, distinguishes Ireland from some other countries is the overriding necessity for economic policies which can secure a significant raising of the level of the economy as a whole. Inevitably these, if left to themselves, to some extent are likely to strengthen the tendencies to regional imbalance rather than the contrary. It is evident that there are, in Ireland, the "imbalances" which characterise the regional situation in most countries, the dominance in industry, service employment and administration of the capital city, the higher levels of income and more varied employment possibilities in this and the few larger urban centres (mainly ports in Ireland), the dependence of the non-urban areas on agriculture, primary industries and tourism, and, as industrialisation increases and agriculture improves its efficiency, a constant tendency to migration from country areas to the main towns or to external emigration.

In Ireland as elsewhere, however, it can be said to be an "ultimate' objective of national policy, not only to ensure a fast rate of overall growth but also to ensure an acceptable standard of living to the population of all regions and, so far as possible, to reduce the pressures leading to internal and external migration.

While the importance of employment in services is recognised, it is the growth of industrial employment which is seen as the driving force at the present stage for the improvement of population trends both for the Irish economy as a whole and for the regions individually. The "problem" for regional policy is therefore two-fold: how to develop other centres of growth outside Dublin and the East, to secure a better balance within the country as a whole, and how to secure a distribution of industrial employment in accord with the potential of the regions and, in particular the needs of the weaker or most disadvantaged areas. Regional policies and strategies are therefore largely concerned with physical planning, the promotion of alternative urban centres to Dublin and the location of industry within a framework of national growth conditioned, to some extent, by the need to ensure an adequate flow of foreign capital investment.

C. THE DEVELOPMENT OF THE APPROACH TO REGIONAL POLICIES

Since the inception of the State over 50 years ago successive Governments have endeavoured to foster domestic industry in order to lessen the undue dependence on agriculture. Various measures were adopted, varying from tariff protection and industrial credit schemes in the thirties and forties, to the establishment of an Industrial Development Authority in 1950. The first step to regionalising the policy was the introduction in 1952 of a system of grants administered by a special body (An Foras Tionscail) for the establishment of industries in areas designated as "under-developed" in the West. This was the area of heaviest outward migration and deemed to suffer from major locational disadvantages of higher transport and labour training costs.

Regional policy was not, however, confined to such areas. In 1956 the IDA was empowered to give grants for new industrial projects located outside the underdeveloped areas, in order to arrest the rising trend in emigration and improve the balance of payments. Other, export directed measures were also introduced, while the IDA was directed in accordance with the accepted policy of decentralisation of industry throughout the country, to encourage the dispersal of industry as far as this is practicable so that areas away from the large population centres would secure industrial projects and share in the employment and other advantages resulting from industrial development.

In 1958 the view that further industrial expansion would have to be largely based on export markets and that foreign investment, financial and technical, should be encouraged, led to industrial tax concessions in the shape of tax reliefs on profits earned on exports and accelerated depreciation allowances on industrial plant and equipement, and to lifting legal restrictions on foreign control of new industries, as well as to extensions of industrial credit schemes.

The system then introduced remained in force until 1969. The Industrial Development Act of that year dissolved An Foras Tionscail and its grant giving powers were given to the IDA. The Act also assigned additional functions to the IDA one of which was "to foster the national objective of regional industrial development", and further extended the range of industrial incentives which the IDA could offer.

Recognition that physical planning objectives should be linked with economic and industrial policy is shown by the adoption, in 1969, of the policy aim of keeping the growth of Dublin to the natural increase of its population, i.e. to eliminate net immigration into Dublin. Although imbalances exist between Dublin and the rest of the country, restraint measures are not in use, the Irish Government preferring to rely on inducements to encourage balanced development throughout the country rather than on restrictive measures to discourage it in any particular location.

In 1972 the Government reiterated the policy aim for Dublin and widened the general regional strategy. The additional guidelines of strategy were:

a) Expansion in and around Cork City, of the Limerick/Shannon/Ennis area, and of Waterford, Galway, Dundalk, Drogheda, Sligo and Athlone (see Map 3).

b) Development of county or other large towns of strategic importance in each region, including relatively large expansion of towns in areas remote from existing major towns.

c) Continuation of special efforts for the development of the small, scattered and underdeveloped areas mainly along the West coast in which the Irish language is the vernacular (the Gaeltacht).

It should be noted that an element of forward planning has been introduced in the regional industrial field. For 1973/77 the IDA has formulated "Regional Industrial Plans" for each region. These Plans map the location distribution, consistent with the strategic objectives indicated above, of the future expansion in industrial employment and are used to assist coordination of the development of all resources necessary for the efficient development of industry. Under these Plans, the planned expansion of industrial development in the less developed regions is relatively faster than in more developed regions, compared with relative rates of growth achieved during 1966/71. The IDA's Plans were endorsed as part of the then Government's regional strategy as a whole.

Finally, the linking of industrial expansion with physical planning strategy involves the supplementing of industrial incentives by an active policy of infrastructural development. Local planning authorities give special attention to the infrastructural needs of industry and there is very close liaison between these authorities and the IDA in this matter.

Thus the approach to regional policies in Ireland has shown a progressive development, in which there are now a number of elements:

i)   The adoption of national economic policies and strategies, particularly in industrial development, to secure economic progress for the country as a whole.

ii)   Within this framework, attention is paid to the needs of the disadvantaged regions, though not exclusively to them.   Regional policy is thus "nationwide" rather than confined to selected "backward" regions.

iii)   The adoption of a framework for planned development of alternative urban centres to the capital.

iv)   The adoption of forward planning targets of regional industrial growth, covering the whole country.

v)   The use of industrial incentives, rather than restraints, to secure a satisfactory industrial location pattern, having regard to the need to encourage foreign investment.

vi)   The inclusion of regional policy objectives in the aims of the main industrial promotion agency (IDA).

vii)   The supplementing of incentives by appropriate infrastructural policies.

D.   THE INSTRUMENTS OF REGIONAL POLICIES

Regional policies are implemented through a framework of institutions and through the specific financial incentives measures in the industrial field.

a)   The institutional framework necessary for the implementation of the regional strategy has been established.   The Local Government (Planning and Development) Act, 1963, is the statutory basis for physical planning.   Under the Act each planning authority is required to draw up and implement a plan for its area.   The Minister for Local Government has power under the Act to coordinate the plans of individual planning authorities.   The establishment of the planning regions was undertaken initially to assist the Minister in the exercise of this coordinating function.   A Regional Development Organisation has been established in each region.   The Organisations are non-statutory bodies, and the planning authorities in a region, the Industrial Development Authority, the regional tourism organisation, the Department of Local Government, and other bodies, where appropriate, are represented on them.   The main function of each Regional Development Organisation is to coordinate the programmes for development within the region.

b)   The system of incentives

The incentive system, administered by the IDA exercising directionary powers, covers the whole country with special provisions for the designated areas. These are mainly the twelve counties in the West and cover 56% of the land area and 31% of the population. Table 8 gives details of expenditure on regional incentives.

1. Investment Grants*

    i) New Industry

    - A basic grant of up to 40% of the cost of fixed assets for new industrial undertakings satisfying certain conditions, if located in the designated areas; in the rest of the country the limit is 25%.
    - An additional grant of up to 20% determined by reference to the significance and character of the employment likely to be provided, the development of utilisation of local materials, the potentiality of linkages with existing firms or potential new enterprises, the technological or scientific content or the existence of exceptional growth potential.
    In practice the following maximum grant rates are now applied by the IDA for projects where the investment does not exceed £1 million, or the investment per job is not over £10,000; for many projects grants are given at less than these rates.

| AREA | THE MAXIMUM GRANT OBTAINABLE IS THE LESSER OF | |
	PER CENT OF THE COST OF FIXED ASSETS	£ PER PREDICTED JOB AT FULL PRODUCTION
- Designated areas ...	50	5,000
- Non-designated areas apart from Dublin ...	35	4,000
- Dublin	25	3,000

For larger industrial projects grants are based on the number of workers employed, location, and type of project.

---

* Detailed information may be obtained from the IDA Annual Report which contains statistical information on grant assistance to industries in the different regions.

ii) Small Industries*

- A grant of up to 60% of the cost of fixed assets in the designated areas. The corresponding maximum for non-designated areas is 45%. The programme is now being promoted in Dublin city and suburbs also, for selected industrial sectors.

iii) Re-equipment

Grants towards the cost of re-equipment, modernisation improvement or extension of industrial undertakings can amount to 35 per cent of investment in the designated areas and 25% elsewhere.

2. Interest Rebates and Guarantees

Under the Industrial Development Act, 1969, the IDA is empowered to make grants towards the reduction of interest charges on loans for fixed investment secured by industries satisfying the requisite conditions. The IDA may also guarantee the repayment of loans for industrial invest-ment. To date, little use has been made of these powers.

3. Training Grants

Training grants may be made by the IDA towards the cost of training workers in industrial undertakings satisfying the necessary conditions.

4. Tax Concessions

- tax exemption on profits for exports of manufactured goods during a 15-year period and partial exemption thereafter until 1990;
- 100% depreciation of plant and machinery in the first year and an investment allowance in designated areas of 20%, permitting 120% write-off for tax purposes in the first year ; (available until 31st March, 1977);
- For expenditure on industrial buildings incurred between 16th January, 1975 and 31st March, 1977 there is an initial depre-ciation allowance of 50%, and annual allowances of 4%;
- In the designated areas local authorities may grant remission for up to ten years of two-thirds of the rates (local taxation) payable on industrial premises.

5. Land and Housing

- Provision of ready-built factories and serviced industrial sites in certain areas;
- assistance for the provision of housing for key personnel.

---

* A small industry is defined as an enterprise employing not more than 50 people and with fixed assets not exceeding £200,000.

6. Shareholding

The IDA is authorised to take up a share participation in the capital of a firm. This possibility has only been applied in a small number of cases of major importance.

E. DEVELOPMENT OF METHODOLOGY

Possibly the most important features of the development of the methodology of regional policies in Ireland are:

   i)   The establishment of the special agency of the IDA, and the integration of regional policy objectives in its general national objectives.
   ii)   The differential arrangements of the incentives system to favour the more backward regions.
   iii)   The nation-wide planning system, including the adoption of targets for industrial development in centres of all sizes (suggesting perhaps a wide diffusion rather than a concentration of aid measures).
   iv)   The linking of industrial development with physical planning and infrastructural development.
   v)   The wide range of incentive measures.
   vi)   The attention given to small industries and training grants.
   vii)   The high "ceilings" for certain types of incentives, up to 60% in some cases.

F. CONCLUSIONS DRAWN FROM EXPERIENCE

A number of conclusions may be drawn from the experience of Ireland hitherto. These are partly reflected in the evolution of the policies and methods described in the preceding sections. They also emerge from the course of economic development in recent years.

It seems clear that the conclusion has been drawn that regional policies cannot be (and are not) isolated from the more general policies aimed at economic growth. On the other hand, the fact that some areas are less well placed than others to participate in general growth has necessitated and justified the adoption of differential measures favouring the more disadvantaged regions.

It is not, of course, possible to draw very firm conclusions on the impact that the policies and measures which have recently been strengthened, have had on the regional situation. In part they have had other, wider, objectives than altering the regional balance which, in any case, must result from general growth policies. The fact that the "gap" between income levels in the more and less advanced regions has somewhat widened in absolute terms does not mean that regional policies have been ineffective, since the "gap" might have been wider without them.

There is, on the other hand, some evidence to show that the relative situation of the disadvantaged regions has not worsened. As has been noted, the underdeveloped areas have achieved a rate of growth in per capita incomes similar to that recorded in the more advanced areas. Some success may seem to have been achieved although an exact evaluation of the effect of regional policy applied is - as commonly accepted - very difficult.

Moreover, there has been a marked shift in favour of some of the under-developed regions, and against the East (Dublin) region in respect of the regional share of additional (net) employment in manufacturing, as Table 6 shows.

This shows not only a substantial decline in the share of the East but also that the least developed regions (Donegal, North-West, West and Midlands) increased their share of a large volume of industrial job creation in the period 1966-72. The IDA's regional industrial plans also aim at strengthening this trend during the period 1973-77 (See Table 7). The plans set out to locate in these four regions one-fifth of the new manufacturing jobs. The record of the past three years shows that a much higher proportion -one-quarter or 14,000 jobs has been won for the less developed regions. The IDA is now revising the regional industrial plans to take account of the adverse economic situation and the requirement of higher job targets to offset losses.

The dramatic change in the population situation (a reversal of the decline over the last century) has had its effect not only in the East and South/East which gained population during 1966-71 but in the less developed regions in which, though decline continued, it did so at much lower rates. Thus the rate of decline in County Sligo, in North-West Ireland, fell from 5.8% in 1956-61 to 4.3% in 1961-66 and 1.9% in 1966-71. Other Western Counties have had a similar experience although the pattern shows substantial variations.

It would seem therefore, that some measure of success has been achieved, at least in avoiding a worsening of the regional situation which might possibly have resulted from the process of national economic expansion. The stage has, however, clearly not been reached at which it would be possible to weaken regional measures without detriment to the objective of a reasonable balance between regions.

G. EXPECTATIONS

As the problems of Ireland are of a special and more grave character than in most OECD countries the case for a continuance of regional policies, in their recently strengthened form, would seem to be well established. If the strategies for physical planning and industrial location are successful some further improvement in the position of the least developed regions may be expected, although an offsetting factor may be the need to continue the process of economic growth even in the most advanced regions (whose income levels are still far below European standards) which diffuses the effect on the least developed regions of such aids as can be provided.

Much however will depend on the effect that Ireland's membership of the EEC may have in alleviating the disparities which exist within the country and between it and the other member States. As a result of the decision by Heads of State at the Paris Summit in December 1974 to set up a Regional Development Fund, Ireland will receive aid from the Fund amounting to £35 million to finance development over the next three years. In comparison to the size of the problem this is not a very substantial amount. National expenditure on regional development will be many times greater. However, it is hoped, once the initial three year period is over to have a much larger Fund capable of playing an effective part in reducing regional inequalities.

Table 1. REGIONAL DISTRIBUTION OF POPULATION (See Map 1)

REGION	AREA KM^2	1966 TOTAL	1966 %	DENSITY 1966 +	1971 TOTAL	1971 %	DENSITY 1971 +
East	6,979	989,202	34.2	142	1,062,220	35.7	152
South East	9,405	319,542	11.1	34	328,604	11.0	35
South West	12,161	452,488	15.7	37	465,655	15.6	39
West	11,338	263,887	9.1	23	258,748	8.7	23
North West	3,321	81,835	2.9	25	78,635	2.6	24
Donegal	4,830	108,549	3.8	23	108,344	3.6	22
Midlands	8,987	234,429	8.1	26	232,427	7.9	26
North East	4,002	169,273	5.9	42	173,811	5.9	43
Mid West	7,870	264,797	9.2	34	269,804	9.0	34
State	68,893	2,884,002	100.0	42	2,978,248	100.0	43
East Region Subdivisions							
i) Dublin City and County	922	795,047	27.6	863	852,219	28.6	924
ii) Remainder..	6,057	194,155	6.7	32	210,001	7.0	35

+ Population density = persons per square Km.

Table 2. POPULATION (000)

	DESIGNATED AREAS	REMAINDER OF STATE
1966	932 (32%)	1,952 (68%)
1971	923 (31%)	2,055 (69%)
Density (Persons per square km.) 1971	24	66

Table 3. WORKING POPULATION

REGION	POPULATION 1971	PERCENTAGE DISTRIBUTION OF WORKING POPULATION, 1971		
		AGRICULTURE	INDUSTRY	SERVICES
Donegal	108,344	42.4	24.2	33.4
North West	78,635	50.1	17.9	32.0
West	258,748	51.6	16.7	31.7
North East	173,811	32.8	33.3	33.9
Midlands	232,427	43.2	23.4	33.4
Mid-West	269,804	34.5	27.5	38.0
South West	465,655	29.2	30.2	40.6
South East	328,604	33.4	28.1	38.5
East	1,062,220	6.2	38.1	55.7
East (excluding Dublin)	210,001	26.4	34.9	38.7
State	2,978,248	25.9	30.6	43.5

Table 4. MIGRATION

REGION	AVERAGE ANNUAL RATES OF NET MIGRATION PER 1,000 OF AVERAGE POPULATION	
	1961-66	1966-71
Donegal	− 15.0	− 6.3
North West	− 15.1	− 9.7
West	− 13.5	− 9.8
North East	− 10.7	− 3.7
Midlands	− 12.6	− 9.8
Mid West	− 6.0	− 5.2
South West	− 5.7	− 2.6
South East	− 9.8	− 4.1
East	+ 2.7	+ 0.1
State	− 5.7	− 3.7

Table 5.   REGIONAL DISTRIBUTION OF PERSONAL INCOMES, 1969 ESTIMATES

REGION	POPULATION 1969	TOTAL PERSONAL INCOMES £ MILLION	PERSONAL INCOME PER CAPITA £
East	1,034,538	533.2	515
South East	324,776	123.4	380
South West	460,410	188.1	409
West	259,876	84.4	325
North West	79,699	25.2	317
Donegal	108,192	33.1	306
Midlands	233,152	75.8	325
North East	172,218	65.3	379
Mid West	267,839	104.3	389
State	2,940,700	1,232.8	419
East Region Subdivisions			
i) Dublin City and county	830,469	457.2	551
ii) Remainder	204,069	76.0	373

SOURCE: Research carried out by Dr. Ross, Economic and Social Research Institute, Dublin, published in "Further data on county incomes in the Sixties", ESRI.

Table 6. REGIONAL SHARES OF ADDITIONAL
EMPLOYMENT (NET) IN MANUFACTURING

REGION	PERCENTAGE OF NATIONAL TOTAL		
	1961-66	1966-71	TARGET, 1973-77, AS IN REGIONAL INDUSTRIAL PLANS
Donegal	3.1	4.0	5.8
North-West	1.0	3.2	3.4
West	4.1	6.0	11.1
Midlands	0.4	5.7	6.8
South-East	9.8	18.5	8.4
South-West	16.8	11.4	18.4
North-East	8.4	17.9	9.0
East	34.2	26.1	27.1
Mid-West	22.2	7.2	10.0
State	100.0	100.0	100.0
Number of net extra jobs in manufacturing ..	18,941	15,256	38,000

SOURCE: Industrial Development Authority.

These data show that the four least developed regions (Donegal, North-West, West and Midlands) increased their share of a larger volume of industrial job creation in the period 1966-71. The industrial Development Authority's regional industrial plans aim at strengthening this trend during the period 1973-77.

The results of the 1971 Census of Population reflect these favourable trends. The counties of the East and South experienced population growth during 1966-71.

Table 7. REGIONAL DISTRIBUTION OF PROJECTED NEW EMPLOYMENT IN MANUFACTURING PROJECTS APPROVED BY IDA 1972-74

REGION	GROSS MANUFACTURING JOB TARGETS 1973/77	NEW JOB APPROVALS IN THE 2 YEARS TO MARCH 1974	NEW JOB APPROVALS IN THE 9 MONTHS TO DECEMBER 1974	TOTAL NEW JOB APPROVALS IN THE PERIOD APRIL 1972 - DECEMBER 1974	% REGIONAL TARGET
Donegal	1,800	2,363	106	2,469	137.2
North West	1,700	1,432	197	1,629	95.8
West	3,800	3,309	2,343	5,652	148.7
Mid-West	5,400	3,387	1,941	5,328	98.7
South-West	8,900	5,198	3,761	8,959	100.7
South East	4,700	9,803	2,612	12,415	264.1
East	17,000	5,482	5,530	11,012	64.8
North-East	5,300	3,212	2,054	5,266	99.4
Midlands	3,400	3,058	1,274	4,332	127.4
Other	—	211	--	211	—
Total	52,000	37,455	19,818	57,273	110.1

SOURCE: Annual IDA Report.

Table 8.   EXPENDITURE ON REGIONAL INCENTIVES

YEAR	EXPENDITURE ON REGIONAL INCENTIVES OF ALL KINDS BENEFITTING INDIVIDUAL ENTERPRISES £m	TOTAL BUDGETARY EXPENDITURE	
		CURRENT £m	CAPITAL £m
1966/67	8.9	270.6	112.5
1967/68	12.1	307.0	119.3
1968/69	15.9	350.8	182.2
1969/70	22.4	412.3	185.5
1970/71	28.8	491.3	223.2
1971/72	41.2	571.1	233.3
1972/73	38.2	663.5	278.2
1973/74	42.6	803.3	361.6
1974*	33.2	743.7^E	469.5^P
1975	67.0^F	1,179.1^E	649.0^E

P   =   Provisional

E   =   Estimate

F   =   Forecast

*   These figures relate to the nine month period April to December 1974.

75

Map 1

PHYSICAL & INDUSTRIAL PLANNING REGIONS

IRELAND

Map 2

DESIGNATED AREAS

Map 3

IRELAND

SLIGO

DUNDALK

DROGHEDA

ATHLONE

GALWAY

DUBLIN

LIMERICK

WATERFORD

CORK

IV

DENMARK

A. THE NATIONAL PERSPECTIVE

In 1950 the population of Denmark was about 4.3 million, and in 1972 it had risen to approximately 5 million. In the decade to 1972 it increased at an average annual rate of 0.72% (above that of Austria, Belgium, Italy, the United Kingdom and Japan, below that of Germany, France and Spain).

The active population rose from 1.9 million in 1950 to 2.4 million at the most recent count. It has one of the highest per capita GDP in Western Europe, somewhat below that of Germany. At constant (1955) prices GDP at factor cost rose from D.Kr.37.6 billion in 1961 to D.Kr. 61.6 billion in 1972.

Marked structural changes have however occurred in the past two decades, as evidenced by the proportions of active population engaged in the three major sectors - agriculture, fishing, etc., industry (including manufacturing and construction) and the tertiary sector (transport, service, trade, administration, etc.).

In 1950, 27% were engaged in the primary sector. By 1970 the proportion had fallen to 11.1%. In the secondary sector (industry, etc.) the proportion was fairly static (37.6% in 1950 and 37.9% in 1970). By contrast there was marked expansion in the tertiary sector, rising from 35.4% in 1950 to 51% by 1970. By 1972 however the proportions were 9.8%, 34.2% and 56% respectively.

In absolute numbers the total active population of Denmark increased by 470 thousand or 24.5% between 1950 and 1970, whereas there was a rise of 722 thousand in the secondary and tertiary sectors and a decrease of 252 thousand in the primary sector.

The main factor behind the contraction of the primary sector was a fundamental technological change in Danish agriculture. Important elements in this change were an increased use of machinery, industrial fertilizers and imported feedstuffs, better utilisation of green crops, less labour and larger farms. Despite the decline in the labour force agricultural production increased by an estimated 25% between 1950 and 1965.

How far the relative expansion of the secondary and tertiary sectors will continue following the accession to the EEC agricultural markets is difficult to forecast and remains to be seen.

B. THE EMERGENCE OF REGIONAL PROBLEMS AND THEIR
    NATURE

   While, in Denmark, sectoral and regional imbalances have been
less important than in many other countries, divergencies in the
conditions and rate of development between different parts of the
country have been sufficient to warrant attention being given to regional
imbalance and to the adoption of corrective measures. Recognition of
the need for regional policy measures has been comparatively recent,
an active regional development policy being formulated first in 1958
and undergoing modifications in subsequent years.
   The basic reason for divergent development of different parts of
the country lies in the effect of the changes in the economic structure.
The decline in agricultural employment naturally affected the rural
areas while the growth sectors affected the urban areas, in which the
capital, Copenhagen, was the dominant centre. Similarly, in the rural
areas unemployment tended to be higher, sometimes considerably
higher, than the national average, and particularly by comparison
with Copenhagen.
   The main indications of the divergencies, following from the
regional differences in occupational importance of the primary sector
and from different rates of growth in the secondary and tertiary sectors,
can be guaged from the appended Table.
   Important changes are shown in the geographical settlement pattern
of the population. Between 1950 and 1960 the total population in the
county group A, the Metropolitan area, increased by 11.8%, while it
increased by only 4.7% in the other county groups.*   This highly
divergent development was the result of substantial migrations within
the country, resulting from the very pronounced difference in occupational opportunities arising during the decade. Also within the county
groups B, C, and D, important changes in the settlement pattern took
place. Between 1950 and 1960 the urban population in these county
groups increased by 11.2%, while the rural populations declined, by
2.7%.
   The changes in the occupational pattern were accompanied by
high unemployment with noticeable differences between the different
types of localities.

      *   The geographical coverage of the county groups is indicated in a footnote
to the Table.   Group A = Metropolitan area;
                Group B = rest of country outside the development areas;
                Group C = that part of development areas where investment grants are
                            not available;
                Group D = that part of development areas where investment grants are
                            available.

Average Percentage of Unemployed Fund Members

	1951-55	1956	1957	1958
Copenhagen with suburbs	6.76	7.30	6.30	5.90
Provincial towns with suburbs	9.64	10.8	10.00	9.30
Rural districts	14.58	17.0	16.00	15.50

In the late 50's industrial development was heavily concentrated in the metropolitan area where excessive demand was noticeable, especially in housing and manpower.

Thus the two factors, of decline in rural areas, with high unemployment, together with the concentration of growth in urban areas, particularly in Copenhagen characterised the emergent regional problem.

C. THE DEVELOPMENT OF THE APPROACH TO REGIONAL POLICIES

The first Danish Act on Regional Development (of 16th June, 1958) was part of a set of legislative measures to overcome the unemployment problems outside the biggest cities and their surroundings. The stated objective was the furtherance of productive employment in such parts of the country which had, with regard to industrial development, fallen behind the rest of the country or were hit by special difficulties. Certain forms of assistance were to be given, applying in practice to all provincial districts with the exception of certain heavily industrialised areas such as the towns and districts of Aarhus and Odense.

By 1962 the objectives had altered. The legislation of that year did not so strongly stress the furtherance of productive employment in the less developed regions but mentioned in more general terms the furtherance of regional development efforts, and of commercial localisation and development which might, in view of market conditions, be expedient. The desire was to combine regional development with general industrialisation policy, aiming especially at export industry. This combination of different objectives under the same Act gave rise, however, to criticism and was abandoned in 1967.

A further reason for widening the scope of the Act was that it had on the basis of experience, proved desirable to give assistance to certain trading and services enterprises in the development regions (including hotels).

By 1967, it had become apparent that certain provincial regions had achieved such progress in economic activity and employment that a further amendment to the legislation was made. It is difficult to estimate to what extent this development has been due to the measures taken, or to the progress of the economy in general.

Up to 1967 there had been no provision for formal delimitation of areas within which assistance schemes could be applied. The 1967 amendement was intended to limit the geographical coverage. It did so by giving authority to the appropriate Minister to designate development areas on the recommendation of the Regional Development Board, and having regard to certain broad criteria: low level of industrialisation, one-sided economic structure, low level of incomes, small and scattered townships, outward migration or low rate of population growth, permanent and seasonal unemployment and limited choice of employment and education.

The objective of the 1967 Act was to counter-balance differences in the occupational development and the development in the population in the different parts of the country, by giving financial assistance to promote industrial and other economic development of such regions of the country where this is assumed to be significant for enabling the inhabitants of those regions to participate equally in the general economic, social and cultural progress of the country as a whole.

The Act was amended in 1969 and a new Act introduced in 1972, but the objective has been unchanged since 1967.

It can be seen that the above-mentioned legislation on regional development has been and still is concerned only with designated areas, characterised with certain problems. The Regional Development Act is not a planning Act, but an Act authorising a set of assistance measures for industrial and service enterprises within the designated areas.

A new Act on National and Regional Planning came into force on 1st April, 1974, and has as its objective the most expedient use of the country's given land resources. As before, the designation of the development areas and the administration of the Act on Regional Development fall within the scope of the Ministry of Trade, while the new Act is administered by the Ministry of Environment.

The objective of the Act on National and Regional Planning is, through comprehensive physical planning, on the national and regional scale, to endeavour to provide for: 1) the utilisation of the land and natural resources of the country on the basis of an overall assessment of the community's interests, also with a view to promoting a uniform development of the country, 2) the utilisation of the land to be determined in a way that air, water and soil pollution, as well as noise nuisance, be forestalled, as for instance, by the best possible separation from housing developments of activities detrimental to the environment, 3) the co-ordination of individual measures taken within the framework of economic planning for the community.

As the scope and objectives of regional policy evolved, changes were also made in the measures adopted. These are noted in the following section.

D. THE INSTRUMENTS OF REGIONAL POLICY

In the initial phase, special administrative machinery was established by the 1958 legislation. A Board was appointed by the Minister of Trade, with power, on request from private enterprises, to render technical and commercial assistance for the preparation of investment projects found to be of essential importance for commercial development in areas which had, with regard to industrial development, fallen behind the rest of the country or were hit by special difficulties.

Further it could recommend the granting of a State guarantee in cases in which it considered that a project could not be realised without State assistance. The advantage of the guarantee system was that it made it possible for an enterprise to obtain loans from sources, such as savings banks and insurance companies, which were not otherwise permitted to invest in industrial enterprises. It also facilitated the obtaining of loans from commercial banks. The system represented a widening of the accessible loan market, but did not normally result in a reduction of the interest rate. In periods of special capital scarcity it might however be difficult to obtain loans even against guarantees.

Nevertheless, until 1972 the granting of State guarantees remained the main type of financial aid to private enterprise. It was possible for direct Treasury loans to be made in special circumstances but, in practice, this power was used only in the Faroe Islands, where the ordinary loan market was insufficient.

In 1962 a new type of financial aid was introduced, based on co-operation between the State and local authorities. Municipalities were allowed to erect commercial premises for sale or lease to private enterprises, and might obtain loans from the Treasury to cover 75% of the cost of the investment.

A further development was the introduction, in 1969, of investment grants made available to firms undertaking investments in special "problem" areas. Thus by 1972 the three main forms of assistance were:

a) State guarantee for loans to industrial and service enterprises;
b) State loans to municipalities to finance erection of industrial premises for sale or leasing;
c) Investment grants in areas facing special difficulties.

Of the three types, the loans and grants proved to offer the greatest advantages and the guarantees least - only 40% of the appropriations available being taken up since their inception.

The range of instruments was accordingly changed and further widened in 1972. Direct State loans to private enterprise at below market rate of interest (at a fixed rate of 7 1/2 %) were introduced to replace the guarantees. The advantages of loans can be seen from the fact that the appropriations were almost fully utilised.

Secondly, in order to stimulate geographical mobility, State grants can be offered by the Regional Development Board to cover costs of moving industrial or service enterprises into a development area. The moving expenses of key personnel can also be covered within reasonable amounts.

Finally the Board was empowered within modest limits to provide capital loans or grants, to cover part of infrastructural investment expenses involved in specific projects aimed at the maintenance or creation of concrete economic activity.

The appropriations available and amounts actually utilised under each form of assistance from its inception to 31st March, 1974 were as follows:

(1)	(2)	(3)	(4)	(5)
FORM OF ASSISTANCE	YEAR OF INCEPTION	APPRO-PRIATIONS AVAILABLE SINCE INCEPTION	AMOUNTS UTILISED SINCE INCEPTION	(4) IN PERCENTAGE OF (3)
		MILLION D. Kr.		
State Guarantees for Loans	1958	1,135	520	46
State Loans to Municipalities	1963	222	196	88
State Loans to Private Enterprises	1972	207	199	96
Investment Grants to Private Enterprises	1969	133	109	83
Mobility Grants	1972		1	
Infrastructural Grants and Loans ..	1972	10	–	–

As a percentage of the state budget the assistance has varied from about 0.5% in the early 60's to about 0.3% in 1973-74.

In the period from 1959-60 to 1972-73 assistance has been given to projects amounting to about D.Kr. 1.6 billion. In the same period

the total investments in private industrial enterprises amounted to
about D. Kr. 30 billion. That means that, since the inception of
regional development assistance measures in Denmark in 1958,
assistance has been given to about 5% of the total investments of
private industrial enterprises.

E. DEVELOPMENT OF THE METHODOLOGY

The previous two sections show a definite evolution of methodology
in accordance with experience of the working of the measures.

In administration, since regional policy was conceived of as the
provision of State assistance to promote development in certain areas,
special administrative machinery was created in the shape of the Regional
Development Board, with powers to make or recommend assistance of
the various types.

In types of assistance, experience showed that guarantees for
loans were not sufficiently attractive to investors, and that loans to
municipalities and investment grants were more effective. However,
by themselves they were not sufficient and, consequently, were supplemented by State loans to private enterprise, by mobility grants and by
grants for infrastructure.

F. CONCLUSIONS DRAWN FROM EXPERIENCE

As stated in the "Re-appraisal" there is a heavy centralisation of
population and economic activity, especially in the capital region.
Given the strength of centripetal forces the problem of regional balance
is that of ensuring that other parts of the country share in the general
economic progress, and that the pattern of human settlement in other
parts is adapted to the requisite conditions for economic growth. The
problem of regional balance extends therefore to the organisation of
the country as a whole and requires attention to be focussed especially
on regions or local areas which require special support. This does
not presuppose an attempt to maintain rigidly the existing pattern of
population settlement. Since not all localities are equally well placed,
the problem is to identify localities which are most likely to serve
as focal points for development necessary to ensure a satisfactory
regional balance.

Since the introduction of regional development assistance measures
in 1958 the population of the development areas had increased by 4.8%
from 1960-1970 as compared with an increase of 4.5% from 1950-1960.
In the rest of the country the population has increased by 8.3% from
1950-1960 and by 8.8% from 1960-1970. The metropolitan region had
an increase in population of 11.8% from 1950-1960 but only 8.7% from
1960-1970.

From 1961-1972 the degree of industrialisation (i. e. the percentage of the total population employed in industrial enterprises with more than six workers) has increased from 5. 5% to 7. 4% in the development areas, while it has fallen in the rest of the country from 10. 1% to 8. 8%.

During the period 1960-1970 the percentage of the active population employed in the tertiary sector has increased in the development areas from 31. 4% to 42. 4%, as compared with an increase in the rest of the country from 45. 3% to 53. 1%.

From 1960/61 to 1969/70 the average income per taxpayer has increased by 201% in the development areas, as compared with an increase of 189% in the rest of the country.

As stated above it is difficult to judge exactly to what extent this encouraging development has been due to the regional development measures taken or to the progress of the economy in general.

Experience has shown that some types of assistance instruments are more effective than others, but also that - in general - development assistance is worthwhile.

There has during the past decade been an improvement in the conditions of the development areas although the instruments available have not been sufficient. As conditions and circumstances change it will be natural to alter the range and scope of the assistance measures and the geographical coverage. However it does not seem likely that such alterations will be proposed in the near future as a result of the development that has taken place.

It must be added that the membership of the European Communities has put some restraints on the possibilities of changing the existing measures, and that it is difficult to say to what extent the introduction in the EEC of a common fund for regional development will influence regional development policy in Denmark.

G. EXPECTATIONS

The development of the methodology has led to a more compre-hensive approach to the solution of regional problems. Since the general evolution of regional development policies in Denmark is towards the integration of more and more aspects of general planning, it will be necessary to co-ordinate the economic and social aspects with physical planning. This will be less problematic in a country like Denmark than in larger countries with different administrative structures. Until now, no formal co-ordination has been established between the different ministries or bodies dealing with planning and regional problems. However it is expected that the recent Act on National and Regional Planning will provide a basis for close co-operation between the different planning bodies and the Regional Development Board.

The regional development assistance measures will continue to be of importance also by filling out the frames that will be a result of physical planning. Conversely, physical planning can be expected to provide the Regional Development Board with an improved basis for decision making.

As the service sector is expected to be the most expanding sector in the future, it will be of great interest to be able to influence, to a higher degree than hitherto, the location of service enterprises. The great majority of these enterprises are located in towns. Consequently a prerequisite for influencing developments in this field would be to focus future regional development action on towns of varying size, suitable for the different kinds of service enterprises.

A few further points arising from this survey should be made. Firstly, in Denmark, as in some other countries, the delimitation of development areas is based on objective criteria, the only political decisions relate to the threshold figures. Secondly, the evaluation of the results of regional development policy encounters the same difficulties as in other countries, although the data show an improvement of the regional situation up to 1972. Thirdly, Denmark - in spite of a big metropolitan agglomeration in Copenhagen - does not have recourse to restraint measures.

Finally, regional development will to a great extent depend on changing economic conditions and on the political wish to maintain the principles of continuing economic growth. These factors make the evaluation of future expectations very uncertain.

SURVEY OF STRUCTURAL DEVELOPMENTS IN THE DANISH ECONOMY 1950-70, SHOWING THE DISTRIBUTION OF THE ACTIVE POPULATION BY COUNTY GROUPS AND MAIN ECONOMIC SECTORS (NOT INCLUDING THE FAROE ISLANDS AND GREENLAND)

COUNTY GROUP	SECTOR	CENSUS FIGURES IN THOUSANDS				PER CENT OF TOTAL ACTIVE POPULATION				PERCENTUAL INCREASE OR DECREASE (+)		
		1950	1960	1965	1970	1950	1960	1965	1970	1966/60	1950/65	1950/70
A	I	36	25	21	16	5.2	3.2	2.5	1.8	+30.0	+40.4	+54.9
	II	322	336	340	343	47.0	42.9	40.9	38.0	4.4	5.6	6.6
	III	326	420	476	544	47.8	53.9	56.6	60.2	29.0	46.0	66.8
	Total	683	781	837	903	100.0	100.0	100.0	100.0	14.3	22.5	32.1
B	I	222	153	134	104	33.6	28.0	18.0	12.9	+31.0	+39.6	+53.3
	II	235	252	298	321	35.6	37.9	40.1	40.0	7.4	27.0	36.9
	III	203	260	312	376	30.8	39.1	41.9	47.1	28.0	53.3	85.2
	Total	660	666	744	802	100.0	100.0	100.0	100.0	0.9	12.7	21.4
C	I	126	93	86	74	46.7	34.5	28.3	21.4	+26.3	+32.1	+41.6
	II	75	83	103	125	27.5	30.8	34.1	36.0	11.4	38.6	66.9
	III	70	93	114	147	25.8	34.7	37.6	42.6	33.6	62.7	110.3
	Total	271	270	303	345	100.0	100.0	100.0	100.0	+ 0.5	11.9	27.5
D	I	134	95	85	72	43.9	32.6	27.0	21.1	+29.1	+36.4	+46.5
	II	91	93	106	118	29.7	31.8	33.6	34.7	1.8	16.3	29.9
	III	80	104	122	150	26.4	35.6	39.4	44.2	29.2	52.1	87.0
	Total	305	292	315	340	100.0	100.0	100.0	100.0	+ 4.5	3.2	11.4
A - D	I	518	366	326	266	27.0	18.3	14.8	11.1	+29.3	+37.1	+48.8
	II	722	763	847	907	37.6	38.0	38.5	37.9	5.8	17.3	25.6
	III	679	878	1,025	1,217	35.4	43.7	46.7	51.0	29.2	50.9	79.2
	Total	1,920	2,008	2,198	2,390	100.0	100.0	100.0	100.0	4.6	14.5	24.5

COUNTY GROUPS: A city of Copenhagen and counties of Copenhagen, Roskilde and Frederiksborg - B other sealand counties, Funen counties and the Jutland counties of Randers, Aarhus, Skanderborg, Vejle and Sønderborg. C the Jutland counties of Viborg, Ringkøbing, Ribe, Haderslev and Aabenraa - D the Jutland counties of Hjørring, Thisted, Aalborg and Tønder and the island counties of Bornholm and Maribo.

SECTORS: I. Agriculture, fishing etc. - II. crafts, manufacture, building and construction - III. transport, service, trade, administration, etc. - in the figures given for this sector are included the number of persons who have not stated their occupations in the census lists.

NOTE: The figures given for 1970 are based on provisional census results.

DEVELOPMENT AREAS IN DENMARK 1973

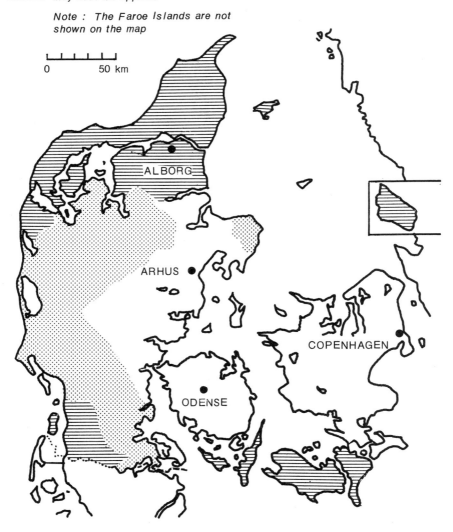

Development areas subject to assistance under the Development Act

Special development areas in which grants towards capital investment may also be applied

Note : The Faroe Islands are not shown on the map

0   50 km

ALBORG

ARHUS

COPENHAGEN

ODENSE

V

SWEDEN

A. THE NATIONAL PERSPECTIVE

With an area of about four-fifths of that of France, Sweden's population of 8.1mn gives it one of the lowest densities in Europe, less than one fifth that of France and exceeding only those of Norway and Finland. The average annual growth rate of population, of 0.72% in the decade to 1972, while less than that of France, Germany, the Netherlands, Italy and Japan exceeded that of Austria, Belgium and the United Kingdom. Nearly half of the increase consisted of immigrants. With a high activity rate (80% of the male and 50% of the female population and 60% combined of the population of working age) it has the highest per capita GDP of all OECD countries other than Switzerland and the United States. In the last decade or so unemployment has seldom exceeded 2% - in 1966/70 it averaged only 0.6%.

While total employment increased by the rate of 3.7% in 1961/65 and 2.6% in 1966/70 there were marked structural changes in the employment pattern. Employment in agriculture and forestry declined in the same periods by 23.4% and 23.9%, respectively, while it rose in public services by 26.9% and 33.4%, respectively.

The contraction in agriculture and forestry resulted from a combination of mechanization, larger farms and a drop in the area of cultivated land. Throughout the period there has been a deliberate policy to keep the degree of self-sufficiency below the level of 100%.

On the other hand industrial employment stagnated in absolute numbers during the sixties. Whereas it accounted for about 34% of total employment in 1960 the proportion had fallen to 30% in 1970.

In the service sector as a whole (trade, transport, public services) employment increased its share from 43% in 1960 to 51% in 1970. Out of a total increase of about 400,000 in the sixties about 300,000 were in health, education, administration and other public services. Since service activities tend to be tied to relatively large population centres this has considerable bearing on the regional distribution of population.

The large rise in the public service sector meant that a growing proportion of the labour force was engaged in activities where productivity gains are more or less impossible to measure. In the other sectors, however, productivity gains were considerable. Thus in agriculture the volume of output increased by 2.5% in 1966-70 despite a fall of 24% in employment. In the mining and manufacturing sectors the volume of output rose by 20. 5% while employment rose by only 3. 7%.

B. THE EMERGENCE OF REGIONAL PROBLEMS AND THEIR NATURE

In Sweden, as elsewhere, changes in economic structure brought about changes in the regional structure of the country and especially in the balance between rural and urban populations. The most marked feature of the past century has of course been the relative growth of the Stockholm area, the Stockholm county increasing its share of the population from 7% in 1870 to 20% at the beginning of the present decade. In the sixties Stockholm, Western, East, Central and Southern Sweden increased their proportion of the total population while the proportion fell in North Central, South Eastern, Northern and Mid-Northern Sweden.

Internal migration has tended to be mainly short-distance and reflects not so much an overall lack of balanced employment in the various counties as moves connected with choice of occupation and careers as well as the business cycle. In 1970 total internal moves over county borders were of the order of 250,000. It should be noted that there has not been any pronounced change in this migration pattern for at least 40 years. The net outflow of migrants from northern Sweden has been one of the main regional problems. However, this outflow has shown clear tendencies to level out. In the first half of the sixties net migration amounted to 81,000; in the second half it declined by some 30% to 58,000. During the first four years of the seventies net migration nearly balanced. It should be observed that the total number of moves has remained at the previous high level.

Income levels vary. Broadly, the counties where agricultural employment is of major importance had the lowest income per capita (in 1970). The level in the Stockholm county was 20% above the national average in 1970 and 50% above that of Gotland, which had the lowest income per capita. It is noteworthy, however, that over the decade 1960/70 deviations from the national average tended to decline (in 1960 the level in Stockholm county was 25% above the national average). In general incomes were above the national average in Stockholm and other metropolitan areas and were lowest in the municipal centre types of districts. (See Table 1). Within each type of district there is a considerable range between the municipal blocks with the highest and lowest income levels.

Activity rates also vary between the regions. These variations are especially large for women e. g. if the women in the rest of Sweden had the same high activity rates as those in Stockholm, there would be some 300,000 more women in the labour-force, i. e. an

Table 1. INCOME PER INCOME-EARNER IN 1970
BY TYPE OF DISTRICT
(Kr.)

TYPE OF DISTRICT	IN GENERAL AID AREA	OUTSIDE GENERAL AID AREA	ALL SWEDEN
Stockholm	–	23,200	23,200
Other metropolitan areas ...	–	20,400	20,400
All metropolitan areas	–	22,000	22,000
Primary centres	18,900	18,800	18,800
Regional centres	16,400	18,100	17,500
Municipal centres	14,800	16,700	16,200
Total	16,700	19,500	19,000

increase of some 20%. For men these variations are rather small, and tend to go in the other direction, i. e. the big local labour markets have lower activity rates than the smaller. High education rates, and differences in branch structure with different ages of retirement, are the main explanations for this.

Unemployment tended to be comparatively low in metropolitan areas throughout the sixties and comparatively high in the Northern and forest counties (see Table 2).

Thus a number of factors, some of which were beginning to be noticeable in the forties and fifties, combined to give rise to new regional problems and the need for some kind of regional policy. The expanding economy, accompanied by a decline in agricultural employment, a marked rise in service employment and productivity and in industry and commerce, led to increased concentration in population and economic activity in the metropolitan regions and the accelerating decline of the forest and agricultural areas. While some attempts had been made in the forties and fifties to influence location of economic activity, it was recognized by the early sixties that stronger measures were necessary and a series were initiated, beginning in 1964 with the adoption of an active industrial location policy. On balance it should nevertheless be observed that the increased attention to regional problems during the sixties had more to do with rising ambitions than with an increase in regional imbalance; it should also

Table 2. UNEMPLOYMENT BY TYPE OF DISTRICT
IN 1969/1970 AND 1971

Index: National level = 100

TYPE OF DISTRICT	1969-1970		1971	
	GENERAL AID AREA	REST OF SWEDEN	GENERAL AID AREA	REST OF SWEDEN
Metropolitan areas	–	46	–	65
Primary centres	171	88	140	93
Regional centres	235	90	176	97
Municipal centres	271	99	207	103
Total	223	74	171	84

be noted that the regional imbalances of the forties and the fifties neglected tendencies that had been present for a long time. In fact, for many variables there seems to have been a diminishing imbalance during the period. This is especially true of the first years of the seventies.

C. THE DEVELOPMENT OF THE APPROACH TO REGIONAL POLICIES

The specific policy for regional development in Sweden has developed in four stages marked by Parliamentary decisions in 1964, 1970 and 1972.

In 1964 the previous measures, largely confined to advisory activity by the labour market authorities and a selective use of building controls, were reinforced. An active location policy was adopted through a regional development support scheme under which loans and grants could be given to firms establishing or expanding activities particularly in a designated support area. At the same time it was emphasized that perhaps the most important means of influencing development in the long run was an effective and coordinated planning of investments. The foundations for such planning were laid by the planning activities denoted 'County Planning 1967' and 'County Programme 1970'. These planning activities, which constituted a close cooperation between the local, regional and national authorities, are

now a permanent feature of Swedish regional planning. In the latest
of these planning rounds - County Planning 1974 - problem analysis
on the different levels will result in goal formulations and proposals
for new measures.

In 1970 the support measures were reinforced by the introduction
of transport subsides and employment grants.

On the basis of the planning work initiated in 1967 a programme
for regional action was adopted by Parliament in 1972. This programme had as its aim the utilization of the country's growing
resources by developing a regional structure in which the different
parts can supplement each other in such way as to provide the people
in all parts of the country with employment, services and a good
environment. The aim was to be achieved by a plan for the development of the regional structure. Four types of centres were included
in the plan, the purpose of which was to specify the functions which
different types of regions and municipalities should perform with
respect to services and employment opportunities required to resolve
the problems associated with each type of district.

a) Metropolitan areas

The post war expansion of these areas - Stockholm, Göteborg,
Malmö - had been chiefly generated by service occupations, industrial
employment having been falling for some years. The expansion in
these areas, apart from creating congestion problems, also limited
the possibilities of balanced development elsewhere. Consequently,
the aim was to curb the growth of these areas. During the last four
years the increase in population of the metropolitan areas has stabilized
or slightly decreased. Apart from deliberate regional policy measures
this is mainly due to changes in the business cycle and in the diminishing growth of employment in the public sector.

b) Primary centres

These, basically one in each county and numbering 23, were
designated in the Plan. The aim was to provide nuclei for services
and economic activities outside the metropolitan areas. To enable
them to develop so that they - rather than the metropolitan areas -
attract a growing share of the unavoidable population movements,
economic activities would be built up in them to improve employment
opportunities, particularly for women and qualified manpower.

The means envisaged were partly to relocate some central Government administrative units away from Stockholm and partly to extend
relatively qualified social functions connected for example, with
communications, education and the health service. The services
offered by primary centres were in general to be largely equivalent
to those in the metropolitan areas.

c) Regional centres

These were defined as places being of importance for employment and service facilities not only for the local municipality but also for one or more neighbouring municipalities.

The quality of local labour markets in such centres varies greatly. The small size of the labour markets make them susceptible to fluctuations and the supply of employment is often insufficient for qualified manpower as well as for female labour.

The aim therefore was to build up the labour market in these centres, though in most regional centres it will remain small, and the range of occupations narrower than in primary centres. In the case of service facilities, however, the chances are greater than in the case of the labour market of achieving similar conditions between regional centres. The majority of regional centres were expected to develop so that they could maintain good services in the future without special support schemes. For some centres in the inner parts of Northern Sweden special measures were considered necessary if a sufficient level of services were to be maintained.

d) Municipal centres

These were defined as municipalities whose functions are mainly confined to their own inhabitants. A large number, particularly in Southern Sweden are situated close to primary or regional centres and they form part of their labour markets. Since centres in sparsely populated areas generally have insufficient employment opportunities some improvement should be feasible by means of public support. Map 1 shows the geographical distribution of the types of centres.

Two features can be noted in this evolution. First, regional planning evolved to become nation-wide in scope. The structure indicated covers the whole country, reflecting the fact that, in Sweden, regional policy focuses on the demand that people in all parts of the country should, as far as possible, share its material, social and cultural welfare. Secondly, the plan is forward looking.

As guidance for future planning, frameworks were established, in terms of population numbers for the counties in 1980 (one assumption being that the Northern-most counties could plan for an unchanged population by that date). In the present round of planning such population frameworks will be formulated for the year 1990.

The central Government authorities were instructed to follow the guidelines indicated by the Plan within their respective fields. In particular they were required to incorporate the population framework for 1980 and the plan for developing the regional structure on the foundations for their planning and decisions that affect development in the counties.

Finally, in 1973 a further reinforcement of regional aids was enacted by Parliament.

Map 1

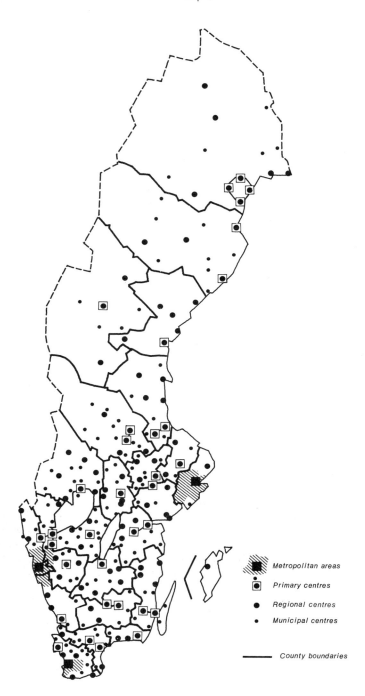

Metropolitan areas

Primary centres

Regional centres

Municipal centres

County boundaries

As can be noted, active regional policy in Sweden is of fairly recent origin but in the years since 1964 it has evolved into a comprehensive and forward looking system aimed at securing a better degree of regional balance in the future development of the country.

D. THE INSTRUMENTS OF REGIONAL POLICY

Apart from the general planning framework outlined above, a number of specific measures have been adopted which apply differently to areas of varying conditions and needs. For purposes of applying regional development aid, two "Aid Areas" have been designated - the "General Aid Areas" and the "Inner Aid Areas" within it. As will be seen from Map 2 the General Aid Area comprises the greater part of the country, covering two-thirds of the total area and 20% of the population, while the Southern portion of the country with the exception of two large islands in the Baltic is excluded.

Regional development aid measures, initiated in 1964, now include various forms of location assistance (loans, grants, guarantees, refunds for removal costs) training grants and employment grants.

Location assistance was provided chiefly for industrial and allied activities but, from July 1973, it has also been made available for certain forms of wholesaling and business enterprises in the fields of rationalization, marketing, technical consultancy, etc.

Location grants normally amount to a maximum of 50% of the costs of building investments but, from July 1973, could be increased to 65% in the Inner Aid Area in exceptional cases and be made available for investment in machinery and tools as well.

In the period 1965-73 location grants and loans were provided to 985 firms and totalled 2,450 mn. Kr. of which 490 mn. were grants. 75% went to firms within the General Aid Area of which 25% to the Inner Aid Area.

To the end of 1973, firms receiving assistance had a net increase in employment of 24,500 persons of which 19,000 were in aid areas.

Almost one third of the industrial employees in the General Aid Area are in firms that have received location assistance. A large part of the remaining industrial firms obtained support through the investment funds scheme. Whereas total industrial employment in Sweden stagnated during the period covered by localization support, employment, as a rule, rose strongly in the firms that received location assistance.

During the period 1970/73 training grants to firms entitled to location assistance were given for 24,000 trainees to a sum of 170 million Kr.

Employment grants were experimentally introduced in 1970 and, in 1973, they were made regular and available to a wider category of firms corresponding largely to those entitled to location assistance.

Map 2

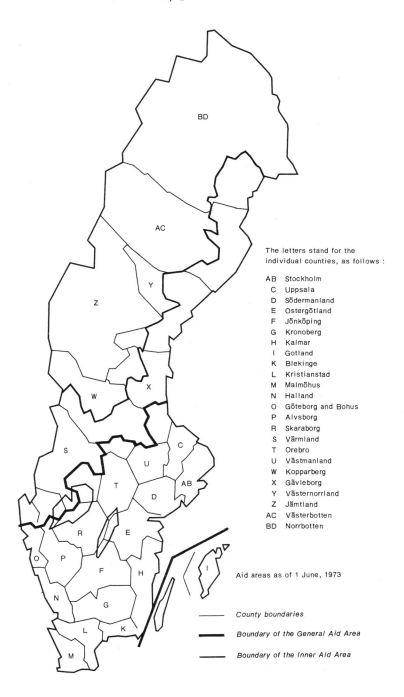

The letters stand for the
individual counties, as follows :

AB	Stockholm
C	Uppsala
D	Södermanland
E	Ostergötland
F	Jönköping
G	Kronoberg
H	Kalmar
I	Gotland
K	Blekinge
L	Kristianstad
M	Malmöhus
N	Halland
O	Göteborg and Bohus
P	Alvsborg
R	Skaraborg
S	Värmland
T	Orebro
U	Västmanland
W	Kopparberg
X	Gävleborg
Y	Västernorrland
Z	Jämtland
AC	Västerbotten
BD	Norrbotten

Aid areas as of 1 June, 1973

County boundaries

Boundary of the General Aid Area

Boundary of the Inner Aid Area

They are, however, available only to the Inner Aid Area. Grants may be paid up to three years, conditional on maintaining an increase in employment. The maximum amount of the grant was raised to 17,500 Kr. per new employee (7,000 Kr. in each of the first two years and 3,500 Kr. in the third).

In the three year period 1970/71 - 1972/73 the total framework of appropriations for regional development support amounted to 1,375 million Kr. The total reserved for the current five years is 2,500 million Kr. of which 450 million for location grants, 1,550 million for location loans and 325 million for employment grants.

Another fiscal instrument of regional development policy is the use of the investment funds system. This is, in the first place, an instrument of general economic policy under which companies have the right to set aside, as an interest free investment fund, up to 40% of pre-tax annual profits. The fund may be drawn upon after five years unless special permission has been granted, for instance, to enable investments to be made during a slow-down in the business cycle or at all times inside the General Aid Area.

Other measures

In addition to the various forms of regional development aid other measures designed to promote a better regional balance include:

i) Schemes to re-locate central Government administrative units away from Stockholm. Some thirteen places have now been classified as primary centres and decisions taken concern about 11,000 employees.

ii) For promotion of infrastructure, which is looked upon as an essential instrument, tax equalization grants from central Government to municipalities were increased by about 500 million Kr. in July 1973, bringing them to a total in the current year of 2,500 million Kr. In certain parts of Northern Sweden the grants will amount to more than 1,000 Kr. per inhabitant per annum.

iii) Industrial centres, each with 150 employed to start with, are to be created in two places in the Inner Aid Area. Further centres are envisaged if experience proves favourable.

iv) Grants for unprofitable bus routes have been substantially increased, inter alia for the benefit of the Inner Aid Area.

v) Telephone charges are to be evened out and reduced chiefly in the Northern parts, by up to 50%.

Transport subsides generally were introduced in 1971 in order to offset the disadvantageous costs inherent in long distance transport from the General Aid Area. The support covers goods traffic by rail and road from places within this area over distances exceeding 250 km. A further condition is that the goods shall have undergone some processing within the area. The subsidies vary between 15% and 35%, the maximum applying to distances of 500 km or more. Total subsidies amounted to 40 million Kr. in 1971/72 and 50 million Kr. in 1972/73.

Industrial credits, and loans to small industries

These, while available for other purposes, are also used for promoting regional development.

Thus a wide range of instrument are in use, including planning policies, financial incentives and support to private industry and assistance to local authorities for infrastructure as well as the re-location of public administrative work. Mostly the measures are of a positive kind, direct curbs on growth of the metropolitan areas playing, so far, a very small part.

E. DEVELOPMENT OF METHODOLOGY

The methodology of regional planning in Sweden reflects the nature of the problems brought about by economic and social change, viz the growth of population, the expansion of the economy especially in the services sector, the tendency to rural decline and urban expansion, and the pull of the large, metropolitan areas of Stockholm, Göteborg and Malmö. While economic and social disparities exist, the regional problem is not so much the disparities between large regions as the effect, within each region, of the tendencies which are conducive to a changing pattern of settlement - the growth of urban centres of various kinds and sizes and the need to facilitate necessary change in all parts of the country. The principal national imbalance in the sixties resulted from the attractive power of the largest cities and city regions - the 'metropolitan' areas. While these are by no means comparable in size with the 'megalopolises' of the large industrialized countries, an over-concentration of population and resources in them could have a generally adverse effect on the development of the country elsewhere. Besides this imbalance the major force behind the difficulties inside the support area is due to the large proportion of employment in agriculture and forestry.

In Sweden the problem is seen as having two main elements: the lack of balance between the aid areas and the rest of the country and the determination of a pattern of settlement. The former leads to the various measures of support and incentives to encourage location to the aid areas. The latter leads to the designation and classification of urban centres of various kinds and around which the most favourable conditions exist for future expansion. To encourage the growth in the primary centres the main policies are relocation of central state agencies and the support of infrastructure.

There is thus a close connection, in Sweden, between regional economic policy and regional and local physical and social planning, and between the attention paid to encouraging economic activity in preferred locations and the improvement of the infrastructure and social facilities in the nuclei centres.

Secondly, the methodology has developed from a policy concerned mainly with location of economic activity to a national strategy for planned population settlement. This strategy should not only infuse regional policy per se but influence national policies as a whole. As has been noted, the strategy provides guidelines which, in principle, are to be observed by all Ministries whose activities bear on the development of the counties and regions.

Thirdly, the policy and strategy requires a system of planning to achieve the general objectives. This is largely in the hands of the state county planning authorities acting in concert with the central authorities. The reorganisation of the County Boards in 1971 had as its object the creation of conditions for a better coordination of various measures in the framework of community activity at regional level. The coordination between the communes, the county boards and the central authorities is done within the County Planning System. This system, which has been in existence since 1967, is now considered a permanent feature in Swedish planning.

Fourthly, the resources required for the policy are provided from special appropriations from central funds - location support, tax equalization, grants, etc. These provide both a framework for planning and a limit on the scale of the regional effort, presumably dictated by assessments of priority compared with other claims on State resources.

Fifthly, reliance is not placed on any single measure or instrument. Planning, financial incentives to investment and manpower employment and training are supplemented by various kinds of assistance for infrastructure and social facilities, and specific Governmental decisions (such as the dispersal of Government offices). Of special interest is the system of alleviating the effect of distance in such a large country as Sweden by means of the various forms of long distance transport subsidies.

Sixthly, the system as a whole is selective. While aid, in various degrees, can be given throughout the country, including areas outside the General Aid Area, in practice it is concentrated in the Inner Aid Area.

Finally, there is a strong emphasis on forward-looking policies, evinced by the provision of a planning framework for population settlement up to 1980 and in the present planning exercise up to 1990.

F.   CONCLUSIONS DRAWN FROM EXPERIENCE

Since active regional policy in Sweden is of fairly recent origin and has been in process of development and change up to the present no very firm conclusions as to its effectiveness or future role can be drawn.

Many of the measures have been in operation for too short a time to yield clear and definite results. Moreover the main trends in the economy have been operative throughout and it is hardly possible to assess the total economic consequence of actions in the regional policy field since it cannot be precisely known what the situation would have been without the regional policy measures. It has also to be borne in mind that the economic situation as a whole has been depressed during the period 1971-73.

Nonetheless there are some indications of positive results. The support measures appear to have stimulated a considerable volume of investment in the General Aid Area which, apart from direct effects on employment during the actual investment process, has created greater employment in the enterprises receiving such support. It may be assumed also that there have been significant secondary effects on employment in other sectors of the economy, especially the service sector. In some cases the total effects justify the conclusion that the development of a particular area has been promoted by the measures of location assistance.

As has been noted, the increase in employment by firms receiving location assistance was of the order of 25,000 jobs by the end of 1973, a small figure compared with the total employed population of nearly 4 million but, of course, a lot more significant for the aid areas. On the other hand it is estimated that in 1970-71 the State contributed by location assistance nearly half (400 million Kr.) of investments totalling 845 million Kr., representing about 10% of the country's total investment in industry during that period. It would seem therefore that the total weight of the assistance measures is marginal but this does not make it insignificant since, in general, it is only the marginal increment of growth which is susceptible to Government influence, and in the support areas the location assistance represents a substantial part of the total investments.

However, although the support activities have thus yielded some results they have clearly not been on a scale large enough to offset the effects of a continued rapid decrease in the number of job opportunities in agriculture and forestry. Over large areas of the forest counties the decline has gone on despite the availability of location assistance. Development in other respects also points to a persistent imbalance between the forest counties and the rest of the country even if present balance should be observed. This said, it should also be kept in mind that a certain restructuring of the regional employment pattern and the ensuing migration coincides with the aims of the regional structure policy.

It would seem that regional policies have not been designed, nor are sufficient, to change significantly the pattern of distribution of population and economic activity which is brought about by major continuing changes in the structure of the economy. The more limited objective, of adjusting the pattern of settlement in accordance with underlying forces of change, while seeking to provide alternative growth areas to the major cities would, however, given the resources which Sweden can apply, seem to be attainable by a persistent long term effort of comprehensive national planning. Monitoring of change and flexibility in planning and application of measures would seem to be essential preconditions of the adaptation of the regional structure to the changing character of the Swedish economy.

G. EXPECTATIONS

The conditions which have given rise to the need for regional policies can be regarded as persistent. The shift away from agriculture and forestry, the relative growth of service industries and the demand for a satisfactory environment and social services favour the growth of urban centres throughout the country and posit the need for a rational and planned settlement policy. There is therefore no reason to suppose that regional policies, particularly the long-range ambitions for the regional structure and the development of infrastructures will be less relevant in the future or will diminish in importance. The past has seen a progressive strengthening and widening range of measures. The future seems likely to see a continuance for an indefinite period of the efforts already initiated to ensure that a satisfactory regional balance is maintained over the country as a whole.

An important change in the field of employment policies seems to be on its way in Sweden. The Government will in the future take a wider responsibility for the employment possibilities of the various socio-economic groups of the society. For Sweden the regional aspect of employment is of great importance. As it is widely accepted that regional development is created by decisions at the central level, a possible change for the future will be a more decisive adaptation of the differents strategies to their consequences on the regional employment situation.

VI

JAPAN

A. THE NATIONAL PERSPECTIVE OF REGIONAL POLICIES

The population of Japan estimated at 107 million in 1972, has increased by about 35 million, virtually equivalent to the population of Spain, since 1945, or roughly by 50%. Its average rate of growth in the decade to 1972 of 1.1% has been about that of the United States and triple that of the EEC countries except for the Netherlands. While the birth rate has fallen steeply compared with pre-war, improvements in sanitation and health services brought about a decline in mortality rates bringing the general rate to one of the lowest in the world (0.68% in 1967) and reducing infant mortality by one tenth of that of the pre-war years. In consequence life expectancy by 1967 had reached 68.9 in the case of males and 74.15 in the case of females, compared with 47 and 50 respectively in late pre-war years.

With roughly twice the population and a total area about 50% larger than that of the United Kingdom the overall density of population of 287 per sq.km. is the third highest of all the OECD countries, less only than those of the Netherlands and Belgium. But 70% of the land area is mountainous or otherwise unsuitable for habitation, giving a density of the remaining 30% of some 1,000 per sq. km, among the highest in the world.

In the post war years these demographic changes and increasing density were accompanied by economic change of even greater dimensions. By the end of the first decade Japan had managed to restore its economy to its pre-war level. By the early sixties real national income per head had reached twice the pre-war level, and by 1972 had doubled again. Between 1962 and 1972 GNP (at constant 1965 prices) rose from 24 thousand billion yen to 65 thousand billion, more than two and a half times.

Civilian employment has increased by about ten million since 1955, reaching 51 million in 1972.

The economic growth of Japan reflects a massive degree of industrialisation, the expansion of manufacture, distribution, trade and other essentially urban services, and a decline, both relative and absolute, in the numbers employed in agriculture, forestry and fishery. Whereas in 1955 some 16 million or 39% were engaged in the latter, the proportion had fallen to 13.8% (7.1 million) in 1972. The economy has also become highly internationalised, importing raw materials and exporting

105

finished manufactures. Economic growth was accomplished therefore through a process of decline of the population and economy of the rural areas and increased urbanisation of the population as a whole.

Population growth has been estimated to continue by 1 million a year in the medium term to 1985, while the primary sector may fall to something like 9% or 5 million. These national trends underlie the regional problems which have emerged in recent years, as the consequences of industrialisation and urban concentration on environment and living conditions have become increasingly apparent.

B. THE EMERGENCE OF REGIONAL PROBLEMS AND THEIR NATURE

Japan is made up of the four main islands - Hokkaido (N. E.) Honshu (Central) Shikoku and Kyushu (S. W.) - and over 3,000 islets. The largest island is Honshu where the principal centres are located. The area divisions of Japan are shown on the map.

Broadly the North-East (Hokkaido, Tohoku/Honshu) is predominantly agricultural, with little development. The centre, with 31% of the national land space, contains 66% of the population and 84% of its industry and comprises the region of industrial and population concentration known as the Pacific belt; the three great metropolitan areas (Tokyo - Kanto, Osaka - Kinki, Nagoya - Tokai) and the Seto inland sea area, the two latter areas comprising the belt. The S.W. is economically stagnant because of its remoteness and very low per capita income. Climatic factors are particularly adverse in the North East and South West.

Within these broad regions the metropolitan areas (the Kanto area centred on Tokyo, the Tokai area on Nagoya and the Kinki coastal area on Osaka) account for only 21% of the nation's inhabitable land space but 47% of its population and 65% of the industry. The three prefectures in which the three cities are located account for 5% of the habitable land area but 23% of the population and 33% of industry.

The reasons for the concentration in the metropolitan areas lie in the internationalisation of the economy, based on the import of raw materials and the export of finished manufactures particularly towards the developed countries of the West, which favoured the ports and harbours of the Pacific belt; in the development of an advanced industrial structure, based on heavy industry and chemicals, which, with the increasingly complex interrelationship between different industries, favour concentration; and the improvement of the transportation between different parts of the country enabling the three metropolitan areas to become the centres of economic activity for the whole country.

The trend of population distribution is shown by a decline in the North East and South West, together (Hokkaido, Tohoku, Shikoku and

AREA DIVISIONS OF JAPAN

Kyushu) from 37.8% of the population in 1955 to 31.5% in 1970, with a corresponding rise, from 62.2% to 69.5% in the centre. Their share of industrial output declined from 20% to 14.4%: Disparities in incomes per head as measured by relation to the national average (100%) are shown in the following table:

	REGIONS	1955	1970
North East	Hokkaido	99.2	82.1
	Tohoku	78.8	72.2
	Hokuriku	94.4	87.0
South West	Shikoku	83.9	83.7
	Kyushu (North) Kyushu (South)	80.3	72.2
Centre- Pacific Belt	Kanto (coastal)	139.0	130.0
	Tokai	100.7	105.4
	Kinki (coastal)	127.3	118.3
Other Central	Chugoku (Sanin/Sanyo)	86.1	90.4
	Kinki (inland)	99.1	95.1

The degree of urbanisation brought about by Japan's industrial development and rural decline is indicated by the fact that, by 1965, two thirds of the population lived in urban areas and only one third in rural areas, (reversing the situation in 20 years), 131 cities had populations exceeding 100,000, while seven exceeded a milion (an eighth city, Sapporo in Hokkaido reached this level by 1970). The high degree of concentration in the large cities was further accentuated by the large number of cities, towns and villages which have declined in population. This is particularly marked in the North East and South West in which a decline was registered in over 80% of the number of such centres, while in Kanto, Tokai and Kinki regions the proportion was considerably smaller, though still between 45 and 57%.

The pattern of movement of population in the 1970s shows that, although the inflow from the country to large cities is slowing down, the tendency of population increase in large cities and their surrounding areas will still continue for some time to come, if at a slightly reduced rate. This tendency has a great deal to do with the fact that the young people who moved to cities in the 1960s have in the meantime reached the child-bearing age, and the reduction in the rate of increase is due to the thinning ranks of the young people who accounted for the bulk of those who moved to cities and also to the increasing availability of job opportunities in the countryside created by relocated factories.

Furthermore, some of the young workers who came from developing areas to large cities in the 1960s are returning to their native areas to avail themselves of the increased job opportunities nearer to their homes, a phenomenon commonly termed 'U-turn' in Japanese, and this new pattern is becoming more strongly established.

Regional problems have emerged from the course of national development, in particular industrialisation, population concentration in the Pacific belt, decline and backwardness of the rural and of the more remote peripheral regions. In the early post war years economic growth, through industrialisation, was a priority of national policy and the relatively favourable situation and location conditions of the Pacific belt led to the trends which have been noted. In 1960 the economy entered a period of rapid growth which further stimulated the interregional flow of people and materials and made both overconcentration and underconcentration a pressing social problem. In recent years the limits of economic development on such a small land space have become increasingly evident in terms of pollution, water shortages and other aspects of the economic environment and the emphasis of regional development is beginning to shift to the promotion of harmony with nature and its limited resources.

Three main types of regional problems have resulted:

a) those of the backward areas such as Hokkaido and Tohoku;
b) the problems relating to overconcentration in the three great metropolitan areas; and
c) the problems of underconcentration and outflows of population in areas outside the major concentrations of the central region.

The problems of concentration are manifested by high incidence of environmental disabilities, air and water pollution, congestion and overcrowding of population and industry, overloading of transport facilities, e.g. for commuters, land subsidence, road and harbour congestion, soaring land prices and housing shortages. These disabilities have been exacerbated by the failure of the economic and social infrastructure to keep pace with the urban concentration.

The "chain reaction" which has given rise to these problems can be described as

a) The national policy of industrialisation.
b) A widening productivity and income gap between industry and agriculture.
c) Regional income disparity.
d) Population shift.

The problem of underconcentration is the inverse one. Population flows out of areas where there is little or no industrialisation because of the poor prospects for a better standard of living, low income and poor state of local Government finances. Secondly, the outflow of population undermines basic aspects of life in small mountain and fishing villages such as medical care, education and various kinds of public services.

C.   THE DEVELOPMENT OF THE APPROACH TO REGIONAL POLICIES

Regional policy elements have been infused in national policies over a long period in the modern age, and there has been progressive development from policies relating to particular areas to the incorporation of regional objectives in the whole system of national comprehensive economic, social and land use planning which is still in evolution. Since the early Meiji period (post 1867) measures were taken to promote the development of Hokkaido and the Tohoku region in the northern part of Japan and which were distinctly undeveloped areas.

In the 1950s, and until the Comprehensive National Development Plan of 1962, priority was given to the development of areas with specific problems rather than to co-ordinated development at the various levels of administration. Between 1950 and 1960 six separate pieces of legislation relating to specific areas were enacted, Hokkaido (1950), Tohoku (1957), Kyushu (1959), Hokuriku, Chugoku, Shikoku (1960). These Acts were concerned with promoting development on an overall and comprehensive basis of local resources.

These measures have in essence been carried over to the present day. Measures have also been taken to promote development of backward areas in other regions with special conditions such as special soil areas in the South West, remote islands, areas frequently hit by typhoons or subject to very heavy snowfalls, mountain villages and underpopulated areas.

Other elements in regional policies over the years include measures for countering overconcentration and correcting disparities. During the second world war the policy was adopted, mainly for defence reasons, of evacuating factories from the large cities.

As the reconstruction of the war-torn Tokyo area progressed during the decade after the War, the overcrowding in the Tokyo area became an issue, and siting of new factories and schools was restricted (1959). A similar situation developed in the Osaka area, and in 1964, the same restriction as in the Tokyo area was applied.

Parallel to this, special laws were enacted (National Capital Region, 1958; Kinki area, 1964) and the development of industrial parks in areas bordering large cities was vigorously promoted with a view to accelerating the dispersion of factories away from these cities. However, plans for factory dispersion at this stage were confined to areas within a radius of 100 kms at the most, and were not conceived from a nation-wide scale.

As a means of combating the overcrowded conditions of Tokyo, the question of feasibility of mass relocation of such government offices as were not necessarily required to be seated in the capital was taken up for study in 1961, and this resulted in a plan calling for the establishment of a Science City to be built on a site consisting of 2,700 hectares of land in Tsukuba district about 60 km north-east of Tokyo. When completed, the city, now under construction, will house a population of 200,000

As early as in 1950, the comprehensive National Land Development Law was enacted to provide systematic guidelines for promoting land development in the context of balanced economic, social and cultural development from a national perspective; but it was 12 years later, in 1962, that a comprehensive land development plan was formulated.

The 1962 Plan

This plan addressed itself to the development of low-developed areas and to the alleviation of overcrowding in large cities as interrelated problems, and, under this plan, the Government sought to arrest the further concentration of industries and population into crowded areas and at the same time to encourage industrial development in outlying areas.

The Comprehensive National Development Plan of 1962 marked a further stage in Japan's efforts to secure an adequate regional planning and development framework. Whereas earlier general efforts were primarily concerned with recovery and rapid economic growth, which remained national objectives (as shown by the National Income Doubling Plan of 1960), the ultimate objective of the 1962 Plan was to promote the balanced development of the various regions, and to contain the growth of the large cities and reduce regional disparities. The Plan was not intended to supersede existing institutions and measures but rather to direct, and co-ordinate, the various specific regional policy measures. The Plan adopted the principle of the nodal system of development, as a means of preventing further expansion of the large cities and of adjusting inter-regional differentials.

It envisaged the establishment of a number of major growth centres in regions other than the already highly developed areas of Tokyo, Osaka and Nagoya. Medium sized and small growth centres were also to be established in juxtaposition to the major centres, which were to be linked by transportation and communication networks. The Plan's aim was to achieve a well balanced development of the regions through chain reactions between the growth centres, and through the spin-off effects on surrounding areas. Major growth centres were to be designated to serve as industrial development areas, or as regional development cities with central management functions.

On this basis the Plan divided the whole country into three areas:

- areas of excessive concentration (Tokyo, Nagoya, Osaka and their surroundings and North Kyushu);
- areas of adjustment;
- development areas.

Very roughly the adjustment area covered the central part of the country while the North and South were regarded as development areas.

The aim in the first areas was to promote the efficiency of the principal major cities by restraining excessive concentration, assisting decentralisation of industry and reconversion of urban areas, co-ordinating the distribution of industry in adjacent areas. In the area for co-ordination the aim was twofold. In those areas surrounding major agglomerations to develop industrial growth centres and cities with adequate administrative and service functions; in other areas to determine the location of major industrial growth centres, as well as medium sized and small ones, and to induce industry to locate in them.

In the development areas the aim was to determine the location of major regional development cities and large scale industrial areas where maximum benefits could be drawn from external economies.

In accordance with the principles of the nodal system of development 15 new industrial cities, and six special areas for industrial consolidation, were designated as industrial development areas. The first part of the plan aimed at preventing excessive concentration of industries and population in urban areas, and at narrowing the regional disparity by creating local industrial center cities. The second part aimed at promoting the development of industries at localities particularly suitable for industrial siting where industries were relatively developed and the conditions were conducive to generating higher returns on investment.

In designating New Industrial Cities, priority was given to' the areas for development' as defined in the plan of 1962 (Comprehensive National Development Plan), while, in the designation of 'Special Areas for Industrial Consolidation,' their selection was largely confined to the areas along the Pacific belt. With a few exceptions, these areas were located in maritime zones.

The combined real shipment of industrial goods of all the new industrial cities during the period of 1965 to 1973 increased threefold. The combined population of all the new industrial cities in 1965 was 10.4 million, and it was then anticipated that this population would increase to 12.3 million by 1970, but it actually increased to only 11 million.

At about the time this plan was formulated there arose a problem relating to areas needing conversion of industries. The coal mining industry which had served as one of the biggest prime movers of the industrial reconstruction of Japan after the war had to be drastically reduced in scale, due to the widespread switch-over in energy from coal to petroleum. As a result, mine workers who numbered about 230,000 in 1960 had dwindled to one tenth or about 20 - 30,000 in 1973.

In some parts of Hokkaido and Kyushu, where coal mining was concentrated, the regional economy was threatened with collapse. To cope with this situation, the Law on Extraordinary Measures for the Development of Coal Mining Areas was passed in 1961, paving the way for industrial stimulation.

Efforts to induce industries to move to the depressed areas are meeting success, to some extent owing to the scarcity of labour in the developed areas brought about by the rapid growth of industries.

Agricultural regions are also being considered now as industrial relocation sites as a means of solving farming problems.

Rice production was cut back, due to the fact that the rate of increase in farmers' income has been small as compared with that of industrial workers, and that mechanization of farming operations produced surplus labour on farms.

Under the circumstances it became quite apparent that induction of manufacturing industries to farming areas will be a great contribution to the development of these regions. Thus, the Law for Promoting Induction of Manufacturing Industries to Rural Regions was enacted in 1971, under which development of industrial parks was actively promoted.

Following the adoption of the Comprehensive National Development Plan in 1962, development of economic and social conditions made progress far faster than originally anticipated, so that this plan, originally scheduled for completion in 1970, became increasingly irrelevant to the changing conditions, causing it to be revised in 1969 in the form of a New Comprehensive Development Plan.

The 1969 Plan

The 1962 Plan thus provided a comprehensive structure within which various regional policy aims were defined. The 1969 Plan however took regional policy a stage further, by adopting a forward time-scale for the period to 1985. It also introduced a new emphasis - on "people's preferences" - by stating that the Plan "must be drawn up with due regard to the people's desires originating from their creativity and inventiveness. Implementation of this Plan requires the full consent and co-operation of local residents".

The need for the new Plan arose from a recognition that the development of strategic areas alone, as in the 1962 Plan, was not sufficient to cope with the effects of a continuing high growth rate (an average of 10.9% since 1962) which was accompanied by increasing labour shortage, increasing size of plants, technological innovation etc. which accelerated the twin phenomena of over-congestion and over-sparseness. The Plan's main principles constituted an extension

of the nodal stragegy applied previously. The characteristics of the
new developmental formula consisted in: (1) attaining greater efficiency in development by linking the various regions with big cities
by new transportation and communication networks; (2) planning
large development programmes in large scale agriculture, fisheries,
manufacturing, distribution, tourism and recreation industry; (3) promoting large scale conservation, development of water resources and
environmental conservation in urban development.

The estimates of land utilisation, population, age composition and
overall development to 1985 envisaged a population increase of 22 million (to 120 million), a more than doubling of the urban area (from 460
to 940 thousand hectares) and a growth of urban population from 47 million to 84 million, as well as an increase in households from 24.1 million to 35.5 million and up to a five-fold increase in GNP (from 30
trillion yen to 130 to 150 trillion). On the projections then made, the
population of the Tokyo region could be expected to reach 25 million
by 1985, that of the Osaka region 14 million and of Nagoya 5.5. million,
or about 2 million less in each case if regional policies were successful
in reducing the movement of population to the central area.

The Comprehensive National Development Plan was accompanied
by an Industrial Development Plan (1968) which included, inter alia,
a requirement that development should be in conformity with regional
policies, and provided for the location of heavy industries relying on
imported materials in coastal areas.

The close attention that has been given to regional problems, and
their intractability, can be guaged from the multiplicity of legislative
measures which have been adopted since the Comprehensive National
Land Development Law of 1950. This provided for planning and implementation at national, provincial and local governement levels.
Its aim was to utilize, exploit and conserve land from an overall point
of view, and work out appropriate locations for industry, taking account of national conditions, and it provided for drawing up and execution of comprehensive land development programmes. The programmes relate to the utilization of national resources, location and size
of cities, towns and farm settlements, location of industry and of
public facilities. The nationwide comprehensive development progra-
me covers each district.

As a means of dispersing factories away from overcrowded regions,
toward which the main thrusts of the New Comprehensive National Development Plan were directed, the Industrial Relocation Promotion
Law was enacted in 1972 and, pursuant thereto, various measures
are now being implemented.

Thus by 1972 a considerable system for regional planning and
development had been elaborated, involving concepts of comprehensive
national development and specific programming in respect of regions
with varying types of problems. Nonetheless, weaknesses in the implementation of the policies, the emergence of new problems, and

changing attitudes to the general policy of rapid economic growth as well as to some aspects of regional development policies, suggest that the process of evolution in regional policy formulation is by no means in its final phase.

For example, in regard to the 15 new industrial cities, criticism has developed from the stand point of both their strategic nature and of efficient investment of funds available for social overhead capital.

It has long been recognized that development of towns in low-developed areas is necessary for the sound development of these areas.

Although a variety of ideas on this problem have been studied since 1962, no concrete project has been implemented up to now. A basic plan for constructing new local towns and cities is, however, under consideration at present, and, in 1974, a public corporation charged with carrying out large scale development and construction of new towns was founded.

The problems for which the various policies and measures described above were designed have not disappeared, while new problems have emerged to complicate the situation. The problems of overconcentration and underconcentration have been exacerbated. Although the pace of new concentration into already overcrowded cities has slackened, partly due to regional policies, the phenomenon of overconcentration is getting more and more complicated. Indicative of this is photochemical smog and traffic congestion on intra-city expressways.

Increasing broad areas are becoming under-populated, with some communities being entirely abandoned.

Such problems as air and water pollution have arisen in the new industrial cities. There has been a lagging behind of social development. Generally speaking, the emphasis in regional development has been placed on promotion of industry, and the tendency has been to expect social development to be achieved as a by-product. Thus, in the New Industrial Cities, far more attention has been paid to construction of industrial facilities than to those relating to everyday life.

New problems have become more conspicuous and will have to be faced in future developments. Opposition by local residents to new industrial growth has developed. Whereas, in the early sixties, there was fierce competition between different localities to get their areas designated for new industrial cities, there has recently been a sharp turn-about in attitudes. Industries requiring large plants now have a hard time finding localities that will accept them. This applies particularly to thermal power plants, oil refineries and storage depots. Disputes over them arose in many areas across the country, and are rooted, not only in fears of pollution, but also in support of increasingly active campaigns for protection of nature and in reluctance to give up traditional ways of life.

The problem of land has become more acute. Land speculation has sent prices soaring and disorderly land development is getting out of hand to the great detriment of industrial development, while land hoarding increases the difficulty of purchasing land for plant sites.

In dealing with these problems, developments are being regulated from the viewpoint of preserving healthy environments. Those under regulation include logging of forests, reclamation of public water and harbour construction plans. In some areas, such as the Seto Inland Sea, which embrace important natural environments, area-wide restrictions are being placed.

To cope with cases where a proposed industrial siting constitutes a threat to the preservation of the environment, a Factory Location Law was enacted in 1973, under which the Government can recommend enterprises to take corrective measures or can even order an enterprise to alter its plan.

In 1974, the National Land Utilization Law was enacted to serve as a basic authority for controlling development activities. This law is designed to prevent wanton development and check the rising prices of land and to facilitate an orderly and systematic utilization of land by drawing up land utilization plans, basic plans for land utilization, by regulating land transactions and taking other measures for co-ordinating land use.

As shown in the foregoing, regional development is a drawn-out cumulative process and is not readily amenable to clear-cut systematization. However, there are two basic laws governing regional development from the national perspective; one is the Comprehensive National Land Development Law and the other is the National Land Utilization Law. Measures taken for regional development under these two laws can be largely divided as follows:

a) Measures dealing with low-developed regions

These can be subdivided into two different categories. For the sake of encouraging development of less developed areas, the country is divided into ten or so regions. Seven of them, including Hokkaido and Tohoku regions, but excluding three advanced regions, have prepared their respective development plans, and aid for the development of designated regions is given in ways best suited to the peculiarities of lightly populated areas, remote islands, mountainous areas and so on.

b) Measures dealing with overcrowding and dispersion

This is also divided into two categories. Measures for carrying out the re-arrangement of three highly developed regions (National Capital Region, Central Region and Kinki Region) and dispersal of industries, and research and higher educational facilities to rural areas are being implemented at present principally under the industrial relocation policy.

c) Industrial conversion area

Promotion of coal mining areas and industrialization of farming areas are being implemented in the respective areas so designated.

d) Others

The following measures ought to be regarded as being a part of regional development plans though they are not directly aimed as such;

    i) Control of land utilization as provided for in the City Planning Law and the Natural Parks Law;
   ii) Specified projects such as water resources development, electric power development and construction of automobile expressways;
  iii) Prevention of damage caused by rivers or sea water.

D. THE INSTRUMENTS OF REGIONAL POLICIES

The instruments of regional policies in Japan comprise:

    i) The legislative framework.
   ii) The organisation for devising and implementing regional policies.
  iii) Financial measures in support of regional policy objectives.
  iv) Public Investment Planning.
   v) "Steering" policies.

Legislative Framework

The evolution of the legislative framework has been described in the previous sections. To be noted here, however, are certain main characteristics. These are that it has progressively evolved towards a nationwide comprehensive system of regional planning, linked with national policy objectives in economic development, physical and land use planning, and the development of infrastructures, particularly in transportation and communications but also in urban development. The nationwide and comprehensive objectives embodied in the legislation are further supplemented by specific objectives and programming for individual areas and regions.

Organisation

There are a number of special organisations for regional policies, the heads of which are Ministers of State.

1) National Land Agency

Responsible for coordinating the national land use comprehensively.

2) Hokkaido Development Agency

Responsible for the development of Hokkaido area, the northermost and a less advanced area in Japan.

3) Okinawa Development Agency

Responsible for the development of Okinawa Islands, located in the southern extremity and returned to Japan recently.

Ministries of the government are responsible for each part of the regional policies.

General responsibility for industrial location policies lies with the Ministry of International Trade and Industry (MITI).

The Government of Japan has established the following affiliated organizations to carry the regional policies into execution.

Japan Regional Development Corporation

Responsible for:

i) financing the expenses necessary for the relocation of factories from overconcentrated areas - Departure Promotion Area;
ii) constructing industrial estates to attract factories to less industrialized areas - Relocation Reception Areas;
iii) constructing cities in the rural areas.

Hokkaido-Tohoku Development Corporation

Finances enterprises which invest in Hokkaido or Tohoku regions, the less advanced regions in Japan.

The Japan Development Bank

Finances enterprises which invest in less advanced regions of Japan, other than Hokkaido and Tohoku regions.

Local governments carry out their regional policies independently, or under the direction of the National Government.

They often establish local public corporations to carry out their regional policies, or to construct industrial estates.

Specific Regional Financial Measures

Three principal types of measures have been in use, for implementing regional development policies:

i) central Government grants to local Governments for the provision of basic infrastructure, mainly roads and harbours;
ii) loans from central Government institutions, and payment of interest on local Government bond issues, for the improvement of regional industrial development infrastructure;

iii) incentives to industry, mainly in the form of fiscal concessions or special depreciation provisions, to locate in designated areas.

These types of measures have been used in varying combinations, according to the type of region, and have changed and evolved with the development of regional policies. The variety and nature of measures for different types of areas in force by 1970 (the time of the Working Party's visit to Japan) can be gauged from the data in the Working Party's report.* (Table appended).

In certain areas to which highest priority was given (e.g. coal mining areas) all three types of measures were applied. In the case of the New Industrial Cities, and the Special Areas for Industrial Consolidation, emphasis was placed on road and harbour construction. In the case of the undeveloped areas emphasis was placed on attracting industry.

Two features in the system then obtaining were noteworthy. First, there was no system of outright grants or subsidies to attract industry to development areas. Second, the bulk of the special expenditure of Central Government for regional development was devoted to infrastructure rather than to direct incentives to firms. Third, the bulk of industrial investment, including much of the related infrastructure, is financed by the private sector.

The new emphasis attached to relocation of industry away from areas of overconcentration led to the adoption in 1972 of the Industrial Relocation Promotion Law. This incorporates two major concepts:

a) "Departure Promotion Areas".
b) "Relocation Reception Areas".

The former consist of the Tokyo, Nagoya and Kinki regions, while the latter cover the whole of Hokkaido, Tohoku, Hokuriku, Sanin, Shikoku, Kyushu and Okinawa as well as a few other prefectures and their adjacent towns and villages.

The main forms of incentives are:

a) Loans or purchasing in connection with the former site of the relocating industry;
b) Loans for removal expenses;
c) Fiscal concessions (accelerated depreciation and reductions in local taxes) for firms moving out of Departure Promotion Areas to Relocation Reception Areas;
d) Assistance for factory building (interest assistance to local governments or development corporations constructing industrial parks so as to limit the interest burden to 6.5%).

*
"Salient Features of Regional Development Policy in Japan", OECD, 1971.

Public Investment Planning

The comprehensive nature of regional policy in Japan, and the close link between regional policy and national development implies that public investment policy itself is the principal instrument for securing the objectives of regional policy. For the five years 1973-77 the Basic Economic and Social Plan provided for public investment expected to total $300 billion*. A high proportion of this (41.5%) was allocated to transportation and communications, (the planning of which takes account of regional policy objectives). Over the same period the proportion of public to private investment** was expected to grow, from 35:65 in 1972 to 40:60, increasing the scope for influencing national development in accordance with regional objectives incorporated in the Plan. It may be noted also that in the period 1975-85 it was expected that greater attention would be paid to the social sector, housing, health and education and to improving the urban environment.

"Steering Policies"

"Steering policies" have played an important part in the pursuit of both national and regional policy aims, not only in the present but throughout Japan's modern history. The tradition has become established that national aims and objectives are formulated by government and are followed by the private sector, under the influence of persuasion rather than compulsion, and through discussion between government and business. Thus the formulation of Comprehensive National Development Plans, combined with the traditional close consultation process between government and business, is the most potent form of "steering". It is supplemented by the statutory requirement of consultation on location of industry (see above) and the power of government to make recommendations regarding location. The system however relies on persuasion rather than compulsion. Firms are not obliged to follow the course recommended by government, but there have been many instances of industries being persuaded not to expand in particular areas. While an industry is free not to comply with government recommendations, legislative and political measures can be taken when problems are caused by expansion of industry in particular areas.

Finally, the new incentives given to promote movement from "Departure Promotion Areas" and to assist enterprises relocating in recipient areas are part of the mechanism for steering industry in accordance with regional policy objectives.

E. DEVELOPMENT OF METHODOLOGY

As can be seen from the foregoing sections a principal feature in the methodology of regional policy in Japan is its reliance on the

  * At constant 1972 FY prices.
 ** At constant 1965 prices.

120

comprehensive system of forward-looking national planning, in which regional objectives are incorporated and in which economic and social objectives are placed in a regional as well as national framework. This methodology is applied administratively through close liaison and consultation between the central, provincial, and local authorities concerned with public investment, planning and programming and with public corporation and private enterprise organisations and firms.

Inherent in this system is the close study of trends and the gathering, study and evaluation of data essential to forecasting and the establishment of policy objectives. In recent times an important new element is the development of public opinion and the need to take account of it in formulating objectives and plans.

The second important feature is the role of public investment, particularly in infrastructure development, related to the objectives of regional policy.

Third, though some measures of financial incentives and subsidisation have been adopted to encourage location of industry in preferred areas these are of somewhat less significance than in some other countries pursuing strong regional policies. Neither in their effect on private investment decisions, nor on their total scale, do they seem to be designed to have as much weight as comprehensive planning and public investment.

Fourth, persuasion rather than compulsion infuses the efforts made to steer the location of industry in the direction deemed desirable from the point of view of regional policy.

F. CONCLUSIONS DRAWN FROM EXPERIENCE

The history of Japan since the period of recovery and reconstruction in the early post war years has been one of phenomenal economic growth and development and of industrialisation on a mammoth scale. The growth and development has led to a rise in standards of living and material prosperity virtually unparalleled elsewhere. In the course of this progress, and despite the attention paid to regional problems, these have become accentuated rather than moderated. Overconcentration in the Pacific belt, with its consequences in a worsening environment has increased, while decline, underdevelopment and depopulation has characterised the peripheral regions. To some extent this situation reflects the policy choices which have been made, favouring economic growth as the principal priority, and, of necessity therefore, the growth of those areas, mainly coastal, which are most favourably located for that growth - especially having regard to the internationalisation of Japan's economy.

It would be wrong to conclude that regional policies have not worked. Many achievements can be noted, from the improvement in national communications, the development of nodal industrial cities and the

planned location of seaboard industrial areas. They have worked
however in conjunction with an economic growth policy - and in circumstances of a very large increase in population - which inevitably
had its effect on "regional balance". The more valid conclusion to
draw however is that the problems which have emerged and become
more acute in recent years - environmental deterioration, etc. - are
a reflection of the regional imbalances brought about mainly by economic
development. Insofar as it is necessary to strengthen the efforts to
overcome the ill effects of rapid economic growth, regional policies
should be seen as one of the essential instruments to ensure the har-
monization of growth with desire of the people for more satisfactory
environmental and social conditions.

G. EXPECTATIONS

Past experience seems to indicate that it is difficult quickly to
eliminate inter-regional disparities, over-concentration of population
and depopulation. However, as Japan is about to steer its economy
from rapid growth to stabilized growth, and change its industrial
structure from one based on heavy and chemical industries to one
based on knowledge-intensive industries, there is a possibility that
the pressure from these problems may be reduced.

Also, the recent decline in the rate of population influx into urban
areas from rural areas, attributable in part to the effect of the area
development policy pursued so far, and the tendency of effective dispersal of industries, are considered as signs indicating the easing of
area problems in the years to come.

In order to solve these problems, it is imperative to take the long
range view and to push forward vigorously with projects for the improvement of the quality of life and economic environment in rural
areas, and for industrial relocation from overcrowded areas to less
developed areas.

It would seem clear however that the solution to Japan's problems,
even partial, is unlikely to be found in a weakening of the regional policy
element in national planning. The contrary is more likely to be true,
that regional policy must play an even stronger part in the restructuring
of the Japanese economy and its urban pattern, and is essential if
social stresses and strains are to be kept to a tolerable level.

LIST OF MEASURES FOR THE PROMOTION
OF REGIONAL DEVELOPMENT

REGION	CATEGORY OF MEASURE		
	(i) CENTRAL GOVERNMENT ASSISTANCE	(ii) INTEREST PAYMENTS ON LOCAL BONDS	(iii) TAX RELIEF FOR INDUSTRY
Areas for Industrial Development in Under-developed Regions	–	–	- on replaced assets - for enterprises with an equipment investment of more than 5 million yen and employing more than 11 persons, special depreciation is allowed and reductions are given on the business, immovable acquisition and fixed asset taxes
Coal Mining Areas	The State's share in the cost of road, housing construction by municipalities is increased to a maximum of 25%	Grants-in-aid are provided towards the interest on local bonds (a maximum of 4.5% of the interest the rate of which exceeds 3.5%)	Same as for the Areas for Industrial Development except that no reduction is allowed on the business tax
New Industrial Cities	The State's share in the cost of road, housing and sewage system construction by municipalities is increased to a maximum of 25%	Grants-in-aid are provided towards the interest on local bonds (a maximum of 4.5% of the interest the rate of which exceeds 3.5%)	- on replaced business assets - for enterprises with an equipment investment of more than 100 million yen and employing more than 101 persons, tax reduction

(cont'd)

REGION	CATEGORY OF MEASURE		
	(i) CENTRAL GOVERNMENT ASSISTANCE	(ii) INTEREST PAYMENTS ON LOCAL BONDS	(iii) TAX RELIEF FOR INDUSTRY
			and compensation is given on the immovable acquisition and fixed asset taxes
Special Areas for Industrial Consolidation	Same as for the New Industrial Cities	Grants-in-aid are provided towards the interest on local bonds (a maximum of 4.5% of the interest the rate of which exceeds 3.5%)	Same as for the New Industrial Cities
Urban Development Areas in the Metropolitan and Kinki Areas	Same as for the New Industrial Cities and Special Industrial Areas	Same as for the New Industrial Cities	Same as for the New Industrial Cities and Special Industrial Areas
Under-developed Areas (with a financial power index of under 0.46)	The State's share in the cost of road and harbour construction by prefectures is increased to a maximum of 25%	-	-
Backward Areas (with a population density of 10 per km^2	-	Compensation for the interest and the principal of local bonds out of local grant tax	-

(cont'd)

REGION	CATEGORY OF MEASURE		
	(i) CENTRAL GOVERNMENT ASSISTANCE	(ii) INTEREST PAYMENTS ON LOCAL BONDS	(iii) TAX RELIEF FOR INDUSTRY
Outlying islands	The State's share in the cost of road, harbour and airport construction by Prefectures and municipalities is increased according to a special schedule	–	–
Depopulated Areas	The State's share in the construction of trunk roads is raised to a maximum of 25% Two-thirds of the cost of school teachers' housing projects is subsidised	Grants-in-aid are provided towards the interest and principal on municipal bond issues	– on replaced business assets – special depreciation – reductions on the business and immovable acquisition taxes